Tales of
TORTOLA
and the
BRITISH VIRGIN
ISLANDS

·

Acknowledgments

This review of the history of the British Virgin Islands would not have been possible without the generous help of the following:

Mr. Lee Platt, Mr. Walter P. Lewisohn and Mrs. Euan McFarlane of St. Croix, U.S.V.I.; Mr. J. R. O'Neal and Miss Verna Penn of Tortola, B.V.I.; the St. Thomas Public Library, U.S.V.I., the Rare Book Room of the New York Public Library and the Explorers Club Library, New York.

The author is indebted to the following publishers for permission to use material from copyrighted works:

William Heineman Medical Books, Ltd. London, publishers of "Lettsom—His Life, Times, Friends and Descendants" by James Johnson Abraham; Routledge & Kegan Paul, Ltd. London publishers of "Lagooned In The Virgin Islands" by Hazel Ballance Eadie, and The Friends Book Centre, London, publishers of "Tortola, A Quaker Experiment of Long Ago," by Charles F. Jenkins.

TALES OF
TORTOLA
and the
British Virgin Islands

Recounting nearly Five Centuries of Lore, Legend and History of Las Virgines, including much incidental Information on Virgin Gorda, Anegada, Jost Van Dyke, Fallen Jerusalem & Many Other Islands. Much ado from The Time of Columbus to the Queen's Visit. Diverse Information on Pyrates, Personages, Shipwrecks, Wars, Hurricanes and Buried Treasure. Tales of Plantation Life, Making Sugar & Rum, Insurrections, Emancipation, and the Colony's Decline & Rise.

by Florence Lewisohn
author of *The Romantic History of St. Croix*
and *St. Croix Under Seven Flags*

Contents

Femme Caraïbe des Antisles de l'Amerique.
A Bracelets. B Colier de Rasade C Camisa
D. Espece de Brodequans.

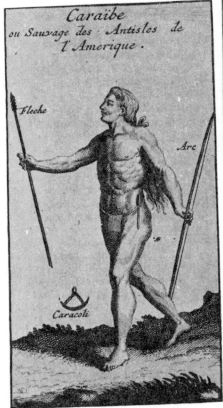

Caraïbe
ou Sauvage des Antisles de
l'Amerique.

Fleche

Arc

Caracoli

Enter Columbus

The history of almost every West Indian island begins with the same ritualistic statement: Columbus discovered it!

So it was with Tortola, Virgin Gorda and the other British Virgins; Columbus passed by in 1493 on his second voyage. We don't know that he anchored here or slept here; there are no signs to say where he passed, but presumably he used the famous Channel later named for Sir. Francis Drake. This Channel, around which most of the British Virgins are grouped, is known also as the Virgin's Gangway, an allusion to the pirates and buccaneers who were soon to follow Columbus through the famous passage.

Columbus, it is also mandatory to report, named these assorted islands, cays, sand spits, salt beds and jagged rocks *Las Virgines* after St. Ursula and her hapless 11,000, put to death by the Huns. Early reports say that the largest of the group, either Tortola or Virgin Gorda, he named St. Ursula, and that for some time the entire group was called The Ursulines. Today the legend of this Saint is commemorated on the British Virgins' unofficial flag, and traditionally the government boat is named for her.

Columbus couldn't count all the Virgins and neither can anyone today, there are so many of them. Officially, the British ones consist of 36 in one report and 40 in another. Old books and documents may list them as 30 islands or 35. If everything above water is an island, then there are more than 40; 15 of them uninhabited.

No one warned the previous inhabitants of these Virgins that Columbus was about to discover them and that their very lives were soon to be in danger. They were the discovered; their history begins in shadow and ends in shadow. They moved up, these Arawaks and these Caribs, from somewhere in the Orinoco basin of South America. The peaceful Arawaks were believed to be much the earlier, followed by the fierce Caribs who dominated the Arawak men in war and absorbed the Arawak women into a new mixed culture.

Columbus found the Indians all through the West Indies. His reception by them on most of the islands was inhospitable, and after the Indians had a little more experience with the Spanish settlers they felt even less hospitable. The Spaniards, intent on gold in the mines of Hispaniola, actually worked the Indians to death as fast as they could capture them from surrounding islands. During those early decades on Hispaniola and Puerto Rico the Spaniards had real cause to fear the Indians who often swooped down on isolated settlements and returned with the ingredients for a big cannibal feast.

Ponce de Leon came to Puerto Rico in 1508 only a scant 15 years after Columbus' discovery and soon was sending anguished appeals to Ferdinand and Isabella for a license to hunt the Indians. The only evidence of Indians found on Tortola consists of a few stone axes, so we know that at least they stopped over or hunted here. Nearby St. Johns island has some unusual Indian pictographs.

By the time the early English adventurers, Sir Sebastian Cabot and Sir Thomas Pert, visited the British Virgins area in 1517 on their way home from exploring Brazilian waters, the Spanish reported that more than 5,000 settlers had been eaten. Two years later Ponce de Leon went south after Caribs and was disastrously defeated.

After this there is another shadow, a blank in local history. The Spaniards, we know, settled for a few short periods on Virgin Gorda to work the ancient copper deposits there and they must have stopped over often on Tortola along the way. Apparently they were not interested in settling it, but they did give it the lovely name of Land of the Turtle Dove.

Soon there were to be more passersby—most of them un-named—the first venturesome Dutch, French or other English explorers joined the steady trickle of Spaniards crossing the Main or sailing in past Tortola in the Passage.

Sir John Hawkins came by in 1542, and again in 1563 with his first cargo of slaves for Hispaniola. He was back again a third time in 1568 with a young Captain along named Francis Drake who commanded *The Judith*.

The Elizabethan Age was soon to have its full effect. The swashbuckling explorer and favorite of the Queen, now Sir Francis Drake, came back from adventures in the East Indies. He swept his small flotilla in past Tortola in 1585 to publicise to the rest of the sailing world the Channel from the Atlantic to the Caribbean which now bears his name.

With 25 ships under Letters of Marque, carrying 2,300 soldiers and sailors aboard, Drake mounted a successful attack on Santo Domingo in a series of brilliant maneuvers.

On the same voyage Drake crossed to Cuba and on north to Florida and Virginia where he rescued the men from one of the English settlements set up by Sir Walter Raleigh.

Back again in 1595 on his final voyage, Drake had with him his former captain, the veteran Sir John Hawkins. Much honored for his exploits then, Hawkins is little remembered today, yet as the first English slaving captain he bore more influence on today's world than Elizabeth or Drake would have dreamed. He died aboard Drake's ship *Defiance* as it stood in the famous Channel on this ill-fated expedition against Puerto Rico. Drake also died before the end of the voyage.

The Earl of Cumberland used the Virgin Islands as a staging area for his 1596 attack on Puerto Rico. He came up from Dominica "again to muster my men, the island of Dominica being so woodie as that there I could not doe it." He described the Virgins as "a knot of little islands, wholly uninhabited, sandy, barren, craggy." This seems harsh judgement on some of the loveliest islands in the world. As the Earl left his harbour at Virgin Gorda, he was urged by his men to go through Drake's Channel but he took another course, saying he was "more desir-ing to be the first that tooke Puerto Rico, than the second that passed through the Virgines." He was the first to take Puerto Rico but he could hold it only five months against the determined Spanish.

Some ten years later the famous Captain John Smith came past the Virgins in a Virginia-bound expedition headed by Admiral Christopher Newport. Tortola still stood at the crossroads; lonely, unoccupied, its steep hills unattractive to those seeking flat lands for cattle, sugar or cotton. It belonged to no nation, but it had its uses.

The buccaneer now knew its coves and harbours. Drake's Channel had become a highway and like highwaymen, the buccaneers pounced from shore in their small fly-boats, called *filibusters*, on the larger richer prey.

THE PIRATES. The first actual settlement on Tortola was traditionally at Soper's Hole, West End, where now the Flying Goose gently puts down bringing in exploring tourists instead. These first piratical squatters were tough, restless, impermanent. They may have been Dutch, French, Spanish or Portuguese, but they were most likely English—renegade English without much to lose but their lives, and much to gain by daring. This was the time of Captains Avery, Roberts, Sprigg and Blackbeard in this area, but no one knows quite for sure who sponsored the first Tortola hide-out.

Meanwhile, other English adventurers had been sailing all about this locale. There are accounts of Sir Richard Grenville in *The Tiger*, Master George Percy, Sir Walter Raleigh, and Sir Robert Dudley, son of the Earl of Leicester.

In the 1620's the Scotch merchant-adventurer, James Hay, titled the Earl of Carlisle, supposedly acquired Tortola and its

dependencies of "Angilla, Sembrera & Enegada" in the Letters Patent given him by the King for many islands—including Barbados, St. Kitts and, just to be comprehensive, "all the Caribees." Carlisle leased his Caribbean Patents to Lord Willoughby in 1647 for 21 years. Neither attempted to settle these northern islands.

THE DUTCH COMPANY. When the first permanent settlement on Tortola came, in 1648, oddly enough it was not begun by the British but by the Dutch who became its first *de facto* owners.

The Dutch had been very active throughout the preceding quarter century in the West Indies and for some years kept as many as 800 vessels employed in commercial and military operations in the area. In one 13 years period they had captured prize ships from the Spanish and Portuguese to the value of 30 million pounds.

The Dutch West India Company had been set up in 1621 and these enterprising Hollanders now concentrated on commerce, ranging from Brazil to New Amsterdam in their fleets of merchants ships. They had learned sugar making in Brazil and brought this knowledge northward to aid the British and French islanders in setting up mills. To the north the Spaniards already had a century of sugar making experience behind them, but they were not sharing their knowledge.

The Dutch managed most of the time to keep out of the inter-island quarrels of this period and acted as merchants of the Caribbean, supplying anything from cane cuttings and sugar mill machinery to silks and linens. They settled everywhere as advisers, traders, merchants and bankers.

The Dutchmen established a small town on Tortola and built a Fort. Its whereabouts is a little uncertain now, but most likely the Fort stood where the later English Fort Burt overlooked Road Harbour, on the spot where the Fort Burt Hotel now stands.

CHANGING OWNERS. Eighteen years after the Tortola settlement began, a "strange party" as the historian Bryan Edwards

9

terms them, drove out the Dutch. The strange party, obviously buccaneers of several nations who were called "banditti" by another writer, claimed to be English and the English Crown was happy to agree with their claim. So the British flag was planted on Tortola and the Crown for the first time offered these islands its protection.

It wasn't long until the French, who were already well established on Martinique and Guadeloupe and who had one foot on and off St. Martins, coveted Tortola. They took it.

The English recaptured the island in 1672, the same year the Danes decided to settle nearby ownerless St. Thomas. As soon as Tortola became British, the Governor of the Leeward islands, Sir William Stapleton of Nevis, annexed it formally to the Crown which had purchased some of Carlisle's Patent and given it to Stapleton. Thereupon, Sir William proceeded to demolish the old Dutch Fort and to remove the inhabitants to St. Kitts. They were listed as being 80 in number, mostly of Welsh, Irish and English descent. The Colonial government did not think a settlement on Tortola worth the bother in protecting it. Meanwhile, unofficial wars were going on between France and Holland and France and Spain. A year later these wars became official. The next year, the English and Dutch made peace again.

However, individual Englishmen seemed determined to settle on Tortola, come hell or hurricanes, in spite of their Leeward Island Government.

There is an account by Lord Willoughby read to the long-suffering Council on Trade & Plantations in 1677 which says that some English from Anguilla had gone to settle on Tortola. He said they had some cotton and sugar on the hills and ginger in the lowlands. The settlers also built some 'works' for indigo, one of the luxury products of this time.

Anguilla on the other hand seemed the island its settlers were most anxious to get away from. It lies to the south of the others, not far from French-Dutch St. Martins. First settled in 1650, Anguilla had earlier been named by the Spaniards for its shape of an eel. It had little wood, no water except that caught from rain, some salt ponds and not much else to induce permanent settlement. The first English there ran cattle and grew a little tobacco and cotton to trade.

The next report mentions that several English families left Anguilla in 1680 to live on Virgin Gorda. Anguilla by then had some French, Dutch and more English settlers. Its title belonged to the English, and the famous historian, Capt. Thomas Southey, brother of the poet, said that soon afterward a "party of wild Irish landed upon Anguilla and treated the defenceless inhabitants more barbarously than any of the French pirates who had attacked them before." Another writer reports it was abandoned from 1672 to about 1700. By this time it was separated from the British Virgins and placed under the government at St. Kitts.

A contrary report says there was a group of families still on Anguilla until 1680 when they moved over to Virgin Gorda. In any case, the rest of the Anguillans seemed to have migrated steadily to either Virgin Gorda or Tortola, bringing their cattle with them.

Old records say that some "merchants of Liverpool supplied them with necessaries for a few years." These merchants of Liverpool were to go on helping out the islanders for another generation or more. They were to hope in vain for most of their

money back, for lack of a proper island court in which to sue for it.

In 1683 England declared war on the French again and later the same year France declared war on Spain, so things continued lively in Caribbean waters.

By the 1690's the planters were making considerable improvements and the British Virgins took on their first form of civilized government. With the capital located at Virgin Gorda, they were given a Deputy-Governor and a Council nominated from among themselves. There were no taxes. Money for public purposes was raised by volunteer subscription.

All this indicates that sometime in this period Sir William Stapleton had accepted the reality of the settlements and had relented about trying to keep the islands unsettled. The first actual title to land on Tortola was issued in 1693 to a Thomas Bisse with the Baronet's signature. This is the earliest land record in the Tortola Register's Office.

There was still some question where the line was drawn between planters and buccaneers on Tortola and the other islands at this time. Some of the most enterprising men were surely both. Legal privateering was a respectable and patriotic occupation during this period, but it is doubtful if the islanders were high enough in the economic or social scale to be given Letters of Marque to go a-privateering.

The new settlers ran their leathery beef on Beef Island, smoked their *boucan* as the buccaneers did, built homes and planted crops, but their small cobles and sloops plied the Channel in search of prize ships as well as fish and tortoise to eat.

About 1690 the English attempted to settle Crab Island, now called Vieques, just off Puerto Rico, to add to the Virgins. Here they found remains of ancient plantations with lemon and orange trees and other signs of former occupants. The Spanish soon sent a detachment of soldiers which put the men to the sword and made captives of the women and children. The English made a second attempt to occupy Crab some 28 years later but were run off again with no ceremony or mercy. The French, Dutch and Danes tried also at various times to settle the island with the same results.

FIRST CENSUS. Another influx of planters came into Tortola in 1700 and by this time the islands were beginning to have a stable population. The first census, taken in 1717, shows that there were 159 white persons and 175 Negroes on the island. On Virgin Gorda, still the foremost island in many ways, there were 317 whites and 308 Negroes.

A census three years later shows the population for the whole of the British Virgins as being 1,122 whites and 1,509 Negroes.

The first North American to enter the local island scene was John Walton, former Governor of the northern British colony of New Hampshire. Walton wanted to charter a colony for Virgin Gorda, but was hampered by adverse reports on the plan sent from St. Kitts to England. Such reports were undoubtedly tied in with the earlier Patent rights to the islands which had been granted to Sir William Stapleton. The confusion over conflicting Patent rights was to plague the settlers for many decades and to keep their land titles unclear for generations.

Walton secured his charter after great difficulties on condition he would put 300 English on the island; this he did manage to do. He became the Lieutenant-Governor about 1710 and set up his seat of government at Spanishtown. The colony, however, just managed to hold its own, for it was the 1717 first census which showed Walton had barely scraped up his quota with only 317 English on the island. His government prevailed until the early 1740's.

Steadily, family by family, boatload by boatload, with or without official sanction, the English gradually took over all the islands in the nearby Virgins group, with the exception of St. Thomas which the Danes had settled in 1672 and St. Johns across the Channel which the Danes occupied in 1719.

A chapter in history which began with the great sea-going adventurers and sailors had run its gamut through the buccaneers and *filibusters* to the era of settled landlubbers on family plantations.

Sugar &
the 18th Century

As the pirates and buccaneers made their exits, the missionaries soon made their entrances, some of the latter being no less colorful than their predecessors. Bridging the gap was a Parson Audain, a Roadtown preacher who seemed to believe in laying up treasures on earth rather than in heaven. He often took out after prize ships to enrich himself and the colony. He was one of the audacious, flamboyant characters who exemplified the changing times.

A small Quaker colony began in the British Virgins in 1727 and the story of this lively group with its widespread influence is retold in another chapter. The Anglican Church sent out colonial missionaries as soon as any Colony was stable enough to support one. The first one arrived on Tortola in 1745. Later in the century, the Wesley brothers' Methodism flourished in England, not without a great deal of opposition, and it soon spread to the West Indies.

The Anglicans took a cautious view of Christianizing the slaves, dodging the moral issues and standing firm on the doctrinal one that a baptised person had full human rights.

The Methodists, on the other hand, were the progressive ones for the times, and concentrated on taking 'The Word' as they saw it directly to the slaves. The planters opposed this, naturally. The Methodists were mobbed and persecuted on Barbados but their influence soon spread throughout the Indies as far north as Tortola where the congregation grew rapidly.

Altogether, along with the never-ceasing warfare in the West Indies, there was a great deal of religious dissension also going on.

The entire 18th Century was a time of turbulence and continual crises. The uncertainties of island life included the communications lag; wars often went on locally long after a peace treaty had been signed in Europe. Today's enemy was often next year's ally against a new enemy. There was rarely a year during the century that at least two of the colonial powers involved in the West Indies were not at war.

The Virgins were luckier than the other British West Indian islands, perhaps because they were never quite as wealthy or valuable as the larger ones and were geographically more isolated. Perhaps no enemy thought it quite worth the effort to invade Tortola when the plums of Antigua, Nevis and St. Kitts were more tempting.

The planters of Tortola and Virgin Gorda lived in constant fear of invasion or of having their supplies cut off, although this actuality never happened. Still, the expectancy of trouble was a way of daily life. Shadowed by the fortunes of war, the weather and the fluctuations of the sugar and cotton markets, West Indian plantations flourished during the sugar and rum era. Fortunes were often made and then lost and sometimes made again.

From the straggly settlement at Roadtown the planters moved out into the countryside to clear the forests and lay out plantations which gradually covered all but the steepest hills. By 1720, there were 1,122 white persons on the Virgins and just over 1,500 Negroes.

Cotton was the first staple crop and the first source of prosperity, so that by 1743 the planters were shipping out over one million pounds of it yearly from the Colony, which still included Anguilla.

The first sugar estates were already in cultivation and the same year about a thousand hogsheads of brown *muscavado* sugar were sent home to England.

Where there was sugar, there were molasses and rum as equally valuable end products. The sugar went to England;

the rum was for home consumption or was shipped to the North American colonies along with the entire molasses output, which was sorely needed to keep the New England distilleries going. North American rum then often went to Africa to be traded for slaves, and the slaves were brought to the West Indies to help grow more cane to make more sugar, rum and molasses. This was the infamous Triangle Trade, and on it Tortola and Virgin Gorda flourished like all the other sugar islands.

A report to the Board of Trade & Plantations for the year 1740 reveals that the islands "computation of natural and improved annual produce in Sugar, Molasses, Rum, Cotton, Lime Juice, Ginger, Indigo, Coffee, Aloes, Pimentos, Turtle Shell, Mahogany, Timber and Plank was to the value of 30,000 pounds sterling." The same report lists 150 fighting men for Anguilla, 150 for Virgin Gorda and 200 for Tortola. The two smaller islands had 800 slaves each and Tortola had 1,500.

MORE HOME RULE. This increasing wealth and stability brought governmental changes, and the Virgins, which still included Anguilla, were given their own Lieutenant-Governor under the Leeward Islands Government. The first man to hold the office was also a native born man. He was John Pickering, whose father was probably the Abednego Pickering listed as moving his family from Anguilla to Virgin Gorda in 1716. Pickering set up his capital at Spanishtown in 1741. He then grossly complicated the defense of the islands under him by becoming a Quaker, and thereby refusing to bear arms. Pacifists were hardly popular in the West Indies where the threat of danger loomed with every sail on the horizon. Pickering put up a spirited verbal defense of his policies and his ability to govern those who would bear arms, so his superiors decided to let him stay on the job.

There is some evidence that it was about this time that Pickering changed the capital town from Spanishtown on Virgin Gorda to Roadtown on Tortola which was rapidly gaining in size and influence. Also he may have preferred to be near the growing Quaker colony at Fat Hog Bay on Tortola. In any event he became a well-to-do plantation owner with many slaves

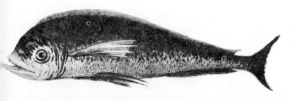

16

and was able to send his sons to England for schooling.

One of the next Governors, John Purcell, was ordered to do something about the smuggling going on between Danish St. Thomas and St. Croix, and the British islands of Anguilla and Virgin Gorda. Too much Danish sugar was reaching England contrary to the regulations of both governments. The Governor of the Leeward Islands lodged a stiff protest to the Board of Trade & Plantations. After this Purcell was expected to clear all ships headed for the Virgins in and out of Tortola.

The islands' first 'peasant uprising' as they called it, took place in 1753 on Tortola, but by this time Purcell, a non-Quaker, was Governor and the insurrection was put down handily.

Shortly after this, England and Spain temporarily settled most of their difficulties, but war was imminent between England and France. In July of 1755, the English issued orders "for making general reprisals" against the French. All French ships, whether outward or homeward bound were to be brought into British ports. According to historian Southey, they captured 300 merchant ships before the end of the year. Some of the particularly rich ones were enroute from Santo Domingo or Martinique. Eight thousand French sailors found themselves in British custody. Naturally the undeclared war was official by the following year.

Tortolans sent a petition praying that a supply of cannon and ammunition might be sent them for their immediate defense, and it is probable that the two Forts guarding each side of Roadtown harbour were built at this time to mount the cannon.

Despite the war, the slave traders were still getting through and the Negro population had jumped from a previous 1,500 to 6,121 in 35 years while the white census went up by only 150 persons. Plantations were flourishing and the Tortolans were still sending nearly all their molasses up to New England with the slave traders enroute to their home ports. Money was in short supply and most of the trading was by barter, particularly for provision goods. Some of the Northern traders came straight down to the West Indies with ships full of salt fish from Newfoundland, horses, corn meal and, most important of all, the makings of barrels from New England forests. The shipping

17

of sugar, rum and molasses depended entirely on the lowly barrel and the skilled cooper. Schooners laden with barrel staves, hoops and headings sometimes carried along a cooper who filled the decks with new hogsheads and puncheons on the voyage down, but most of the larger Estates trained their own coopers.

JUSTICE AND INJUSTICE. By mid-century the colonists felt strong enough to ask for more local authority in their civil government and for Constitutional Courts of Justice separate from those of the Leeward islands.

But trouble was looming. "The provincial court appointed for the ease and benefit of the merchants and the people in general by the management of some few self-interested individuals became an engine of injustice and oppression to the people, as may be collected from the minutes of their proceedings in the secretary's office at Tortola."

This protest was from George Suckling, a lawyer writing many years later in lawyer's language, pleading for a real cleanup of Tortolan politics. Suckling was reviewing the history of the situation which had existed long before he arrived.

Of this earlier period he said, "Nothing appeared to be of sufficient importance to revive the 'sinking credit' of the inhabitants, but the establishment of some permanent laws, which should give at once security to property, and enable the creditor to recover his just demands, where honour and virtue had not a sufficient efficiency to discharge the obligations."

Translated, this meant that the sometimes well-off planters in the Virgins had lost their credit with the Liverpool merchants, who had first helped the previous generation when they moved to Virgin Gorda and Tortola from Anguilla, and who had continued to help their sons and newcomers. It took a huge capital investment to start a sugar plantation, and once started it was often a gamble whether the owner could hold out long enough during bad years of war and drought to pay off creditors. Most of the planters were honest enough, but high and opulent living added to the problems of some of them. As Suckling put it, "some wouldn't and some couldn't pay."

"The 'virtuous colonists'," he said, "began to entertain

18

serious hopes that the British government would place them on an equal footing with the neighboring islands, by establishing among them Constitutional Courts of Justice, and by giving them civil government which would rescue them from their dependent state; with this request, they promised themselves a revival of their 'wounded' credit, and a discharge of their public debts. These first requests to the British government were made in 1756."

Suckling viewed these early attempts of the 'virtuous' colonists as machinations to avoid their private debts and revive their private 'wounded credit.' He has some dryly harsh words for what he felt was an evasion of responsibilities. However, His Majesty turned down the 1756 request and it was not until many years later that part of the political demands were granted.

In spite of all the problems, trade continued to grow as the figures for exports from the Virgins in 1770 show: to the value of £61,696 to Great Britain and to North America, £10,132.

The planters' 'wounded credit' must have expired entirely in 1772—the year of the "worst hurricane in the memory of man." There are no eye-witness reports from Tortola, but the English *Annual Register* for that year and the *Sailor's Hornbook* reported that the sea at nearby St. Croix rose 70 feet above normal and carried away 460 houses at Christiansted and all but three houses at Frederiksted. The damage was estimated at $5,000,000. Tortola probably got off a little easier since it is generally a higher island, but the mighty storm must have ruined the cane and cotton fields and many of the sugar works.

FIRST ASSEMBLY CONVENES. Two years later the first Assembly or Legislature for the Virgin Islands convened at Tortola. This was cause for jubilation. The planters had again presented an importunate plea to His Majesty recounting their troubles, dangers, their need to raise taxes to pay clergymen, erect jails, build churches, erect forts and to make their own laws. In return for which privileges they were willing to grant the King a 4½ per centum of all export values. The arrangement went through and after almost 20 years of hoping, the planters now had their own Assembly of 12 members, all appointed by the Governor.

They had their Assembly but still no Constitutional Court, so the Assemblymen acted as judges, jury and police supervisors. It was still four years before lawyer Suckling would arrive to try to set up the official Court, which he indicates the Assembly only pretended to want. He later wrote that this first Assembly knew little of English law or of its constitution, and that those in debt were not likely to consent to enact laws which would enable their creditors to sue!

Suckling reserved a few kind words for the ladies. He found their "behavior is polite and their conversation entertaining, sprightly, but very delicate and modest; their dress is very neat, but not gaudy . . . they have a tender manner of treating their servants and slaves . . . no people in the West Indies are better obeyed than they."

The new Assembly became full of delays and evasions. The members and planters badly wanted a Title to Land bill which would settle many old issues concerning land grants under Patents. In the earlier days these grants sometimes overlapped when those given by one King were retracted or ignored by the next. Patents were sold, leased, lapsed and sometimes returned to the Crown.

Without a Constitutional Court the islanders couldn't get a Title Act to work, but with a Court they could be sued by all those merchants who had staked them or their parents in setting up their sugar and cotton Estates. It was quite a dilemma, but more urgent matters intervened.

1776. The shot heard 'round the world' from Massachusetts was heard loud and clear in the West Indies. The initial effect was recorded by historian Southey who wrote that soon "in consequence of the American war, several of the articles used for the support of Negroes in the West Indies rose to four times their customary price. Great distress was felt in the islands...." Also the price of barrel hoops, staves and headings spiralled.

The West Indian colonists were caught in the middle. Their loyalties lay with England but often their sympathies and their needs lay with the northern colonies. The West Indian, too, had at times been subject to "taxation without representation" and had chafed under restrictive trade laws. The West Indies had equal cause to protest restrictions set up by the Board of Trade & Plantations.

The northern colonists sought aid from the West Indies and unofficially they got a great deal on a private basis. After all, the West Indians really didn't believe that their northern cousins would ever win their revolution—but they might win a few good concessions from George III and these might help all the colonies. Nor did the West Indians have a continent to draw on if they should want to join the northern cause. All in all, realism prevailed and the West Indians never seriously considered going to war against their King.

Down the line from Tortola, the little Dutch free port island of St. Eustatius became temporarily the richest port in the world, acting as a trans-shipment point for goods sent up to North America. Some of the supplies originated in Europe, but much came right from the local English, Dutch, French and Danish islands.

From the St. Eustatius Fort was fired the first salute to the the new Stars & Stripes, and this daring and indiscreet act greatly enraged the English government.

Finally St. Eustatius became such a sore point with Britain that Admiral Rodney swooped down on the neutral island, before the Dutch Governor knew what was going on, capturing every ship in the harbour. These included quite a number of English merchant ships full of contraband bound for North America.

Rodney, using the exigencies of war as his excuse, held a gigantic auction of ships and goods sold to friendly and enemy buyers alike to the value of some $25,000,000. Ships of many nations were involved, some of them quite neutral nations. The upshot was an impressive maze of law suits later in Admiralty Court. Strong-minded Rodney had nothing but scorn for his fellow-English living on St. Eustatius who protested the selling of their private property.

The whole affair took on a slightly comic opera air. Rodney insisted before an investigation committee of the House of Commons that these goods were of an illegal and contraband nature. The Dutch Governor of St. Eustatius was sent to England and tried for high treason for corresponding with American representative, Samuel Adams, at The Hague and for furnishing America with military stores and ammunition.

While Rodney's *coup* had been effective in destroying "the nest of vipers" which he declared lurked there, he neglected to leave enough garrison at St. Eustatius. The French soon took the island with a tiny force and for their ingenuity got two million *livres* in auction money and goods. Then other French ships captured the English convoy which was carrying home some of the money from the auction and some of the unsold prize vessels.

It soon became every nation and every island for itself in this period. The West Indies was equivalent to a second front for the American Revolution. And long after the Revolution was over in North America, the French and English fought on in the Caribbean in an aftermath of conflicts which dragged on for several years. Warships prowled the seas, and land battles devastated many towns. Islands changed hands with monotonous regularity.

LITTLE LAW AND NO ORDER. In the midst of all this, George Suckling finally arrived at Tortola in 1778, ready to be Chief Justice of the Virgin Islands. He had secured his post two years earlier through Lord George Germain, Secretary of State for The American Department. Suckling sailed out confidently with his family after two years of waiting for his official commission to establish the Court of Constitutional Justice. Believing that the island Assembly had already passed its Court Act and that his Commission would soon follow, lawyer Suckling came ahead.

He found the inhabitants "in a state of lawless ferment. Life, liberty and property were hourly exposed to the insults and depredations of the riotous and lawless. The authority of His Majesty's Council, as conservators of the peace, was defied and ridiculed, for want of a proper prison to confine offenders.... a little walled cellar had been used."

Judge Suckling found to his astonishment that the legal

procedure was such that it was harder to get prisoners out of the little cellar than in. He discovered two unhappy men there who had been confined for some years "without bail, without trial, without condemnation, and without any hope of deliverance." There was no court-house for the transaction of public business; fraud was practiced with impunity. "The indolent and base preyed upon the vitals of the industrious and virtuous."

"Private credit sunk with the invasion of private property. There was no law to compel the payment of debts. In the midst of these evils, a general scarcity of every necessary article of life aggravated the various ills."

"The island presented a shocking scene of anarchy; miserable indeed, and disgraceful to government, not to be equalled in any other of His Majesty's dominions, or perhaps in any civilized country in the world."

What to do about it? The would-be Chief Justice set about making some reforms, but he was blocked at every turn, still lacking his Royal Commission. He blamed the local situation on those leading citizens, who for their own private ends had aided in establishing a separate government for the Virgin Islands. Some of them were large plantation owners, up to their ears in debt.

The Assembly members still wanted their Title Act, but they would not pass the Court Bill for fear of creditors. The Chief Justice was hamstrung. After 14 weeks of waiting for his salary and expenses from London he had to sell his furniture and books. In desperation, he left the Colony for London to plead his case, not waiting for a proper leave of absence permit. He found himself preceded by an Agent in London sent over by the Council who effectively undermined him. Even at this early date the vested interests had learned the value of a good public relations man on the spot at the right moment.

Suckling found he had lost the support of his patron, Lord George Germain; his salary and expenses were 20 months in arrears. Finally he was offered a Treasury Order for it all, to be paid out of Tortola's 4½ per centum to the King, but not to be paid for 18 more months unless he would take a 20% discount, which he refused to do.

Feeling strongly the injustice of it all, Suckling took recourse to publicity. In 1780 he wrote his case history of the situation and his mis-adventures on Tortola and had it published.

At one point during his time there, Suckling said that two-thirds of the people on Tortola were law-abiding, loyal and industrious. Among those must have been members of the dwindling Quaker colony, for it was the year he arrived that the Nottinghams freed their slaves and gave them Estate Long Look. The influence of the Quakers had about died out and the lawless element predominated over the law-abiding.

BUSINESS AS USUAL. The planters tried to keep on with their sugar, rum and molasses making during all the times of internal dissension and war scares. The economic reports for these years vary greatly, but the West Indian historian Bryan Edwards says that by 1787 there were some 40 ships sent from Tortola to Great Britain, bearing produce to the value of over £166,000. Cotton was still the leading export over sugar. Edwards comments that the island still had no fixed local taxes and raised public works money by subscription.

Next year's report of the English Privy Council lists 9,000 slaves for the British Virgins and adds that the Patented Estates were taxed from England to the sum of £25,000.

The British Virgins stood that year of 1787 at the bottom of the economic list with the lowest valuation of all the British West Indies, yet they had 9,000 slaves valued at £40 each.

The British were still exporting about 38,000 slaves annually from Africa. Tortola actually accounted for very little of this traffic but its shipment of 6,100 hogsheads of sugar in 1789 indicates that the plantations were doing better than in the previous decade.

Daily life was still being lived precariously to the tune of danger and local warfare. The century rounded off with a succinct report that in 1798 the British took 99 privateers, of which 89 were French. As France's help to the North Americans had involved her in a long-drawn out war with the English in Caribbean waters, so now the Napoleonic Wars were about to further change the course of West Indian history.

Plantation Life

The myth of the opulent life on an old West Indian sugar plantation has been perpetuated for two centuries, but when examined closely, particularly in relation to the Virgin Islands, the myth seldom holds up. The way of life often brought wealth and position but just as often it ended in misfortune and failure. A sugar plantation was unlike any other sort and in many ways such estates on Tortola or Virgin Gorda were unlike those on the larger, wealthier islands.

For a brief span of time the sugar barons ruled the West Indian roost: each strove to emulate his peers or his superiors, yet each was subject to failure and bankruptcy from mounting debts caused by the calamaties of wars, droughts and hurricanes. The actualities of daily life were ones of strange contradictions, with one reality always uppermost: it was slave labor which was the backbone of the system. Later, after Emancipation, some of the planters found much to their surprise that they could run a plantation efficiently with freed, paid labor.

When times were good they brought luxury, and when they were bad they brought disaster. The Quaker physician John Coakley Lettsom, on coming out from London in 1767 found Tortola just pulling out of a slump and into very good sugar years. The planters, he said, "were rolling in gold; slaves were worth 60 to 100 pounds each." Ex-Governor John Pickering had over 500 slaves, and Bezaliel Hodge, the wealthiest of all had 1,000. But these were the exceptions; there were probably not more than a dozen truly rich planters on Tortola and a dozen more who could qualify for the well-off bracket. Still, the historian Bryan Edwards, calculated that a slave's work at this time brought in around £25 profit per year for his master. He was speaking also of cotton estates.

Our most realistic descriptions of plantation life on Tortola come through the pens of the travelling writers of the period who came out from England or down from the northern colonies and felt the urge to have their impressions published. They found each plantation a self-contained unit, functioning as a separate community similar to a village. It was never quite self-sufficient, but always dependent on vital supplies from off the island.

The visitors rode through the island amid fields of waving green sugar cane or cotton, which on Tortola grew up and down hill oftener than on the level and filled the valleys, too, as far as the eye could see.

THE ESTATE. The plantation's Greathouse or family dwelling usually stood on a knoll with a view of the sea or the fields below, and it was in style to have an impressive double row of mahogany, tamarind or tibet trees border the carriage road. The mansion was usually built with a lower floor of mortared brick and stone; the walls were sometimes two feet thick and plastered inside. The upper floor was often made of wood, and there were wide galleries around the house, sometimes on both levels. Everything was as open as possible to provide for natural air conditioning from the trade winds.

The house design was simple but dignified by large rooms with high ceilings. The windows were deeply recessed and each had its shutters and massive iron bars ready for hurricanes.

The interior consisted of a great hall for living and entertaining, a dining salon, serving gallery and bedrooms. The more pretentious Greathouses sometimes had a ballroom. Somewhere near the rear door was the completely separate cookhouse, again made of mortared stone and brick. A huge chimney rose from the enormous fireplace or stove area and the bake ovens. Tropical cooks rarely worked over an open fireplace. Instead, across one whole end of the cookhouse was a built-in bank of cookpots or grills with a flat top and four or five square openings much like the burners on a modern stove. Each of these had it own separate fire fed from openings below. This system was cooler than open hearth cooking and provided more flexibility. To the side of the chimney were two or more bake ovens. Often there were auxiliary separate clay cookpots shaped to hold charcoal below and one large iron pot above, which could be moved to cook anywhere.

Cookhouse furnishings included a big worktable, churns, all sizes of iron pots, teakettles, pewter or wood serving plates, wooden mixing trays and bowls, drying racks for herbs, equipment for candle-making, a mesh covered cooler for food storage, and all the miscellaneous tinware, brass and copper utensils needed.

Somewhere near the cookhouse stood the drip-stone shelter which covered a hollowed out limestone through which water seeped for purification. Another drip-stone often stood on a side gallery of the Greathouse for handy family use.

The separate bathhouse with its tin tub or one built in of mortar stood back of the Greathouse. Here the slaves brought the buckets of water, hot or cold, fresh or salt, used for bathing. Water was always a problem and every possible roof area was guttered to send the rain into cisterns near or under each building. On Tortola these were usually above-ground because of the rocky hilltops. They were built of stone and mortar in a rectangular shape with a domed roof. Cisterns of this type can be seen today in the backyards of Roadtown where their two-foot thick walls have been keeping water cool and pure for perhaps two hundred years or more.

Inside the Greathouse the furniture, linens, glasswear and other luxuries were as elaborate as the planter could afford. Everything possible came from Europe, although some lovely hardwood furniture was made on the islands closely copying the European styles of the day. Bedrooms had massive commodes, huge four-posters and comfortable mahogany rockers. The glistening dining table of mahogany, teak, fruitwood or tibet was the Mistress's pride. On it she set the the finest of Madeira laces, the goblets and wines of France, and her pewter or silver from England. The furnishings were often finer than the food on Tortola, as supplies were limited, ships delayed, prices high, pro-

SUGAR BOILING.

visions sometimes difficult to grow and local foods not always to the cultivated tastes of the planters.

The Mistress presided over a large ménage of house and garden or yard servants. She was the purveyor of culture and the representative of the leisured class. Yet on Tortola and Virgin Gorda she often needed the qualities of a pioneer woman and the ingenuity not generally associated with her ladylike education. Despite the climate she clung tenaciously to her hoops and crinolines, shawls and boots (which came in handy for the mud), her tea gowns, her ballgown from London or Paris, and above all, her sunshade.

The Mistress needed to be a good horsewoman if she hoped to make her rounds of calls on Tortola, as it had few carriage roads except on the flat coastal areas near Roadtown.

Contrasted with the air of leisure and languid torpor of the Greathouse, at some distance was situated the bustling, noisy sugar works. This was usually built on a hillside or another knoll with the grinding mill on top and the boiling sheds downhill from this. Here the Master spent much of his time when he wasn't worrying over the plantation account books.

Any planter hopeful of success was a hard-working man who often put in dawn-to-dusk hours broken only by a mid-day siesta after dinner. True he had managers, overseers, drivers and a whole bevy of assistants, but he was foremost an administrator who had his own duties. Those who left the estate supervision to less self-interested persons soon found themselves in debt or Chancery Court.

Near the boiling house was the molasses cistern where the

hogsheads of sugar drained, and near this was built the rum stillhouse and pot still. There were also nearby stables, storehouses, a hospital or sick-house and the dwellings for the manager and overseers.

Not far away stood the rows of slave huts usually built in early-motel style with one row facing another. Near this Village, as it was called, lay the workers' own provision grounds where they might grow what they pleased. Pasture land was also alloted for their cattle and other animals, and for those of the planter. Except for these areas necessary for living, working and growing provisions, almost every other acre went into sugar cane or cotton cultivation. Some fortunate planters had good forests on their estates for use as timbers and firewood. Each estate burned its own charcoal in a large fire pit.

THE SUGAR SEASON. The production of sugar was a long, complex procedure, calling for a large investment in land, machinery and labor. The canes were planted by hand from cuttings, each put into a carefully prepared hole. Holing at best was hard, back-breaking work in the sun on the level ground. At worst, as on hilly Tortola, the workers had to form terraces and make embankments with field stones. Then the trench was made two feet deep and three wide from ridge to ridge.

Once planted a cane field re-newed or 'ratooned' itself with new growth after each crop for about five years depending on the soil and its care. Planters kept enough fields in rotation so that the field hands had work during the growing season each year.

At early dawn the workers streamed out of the Village when the slave Driver blew the conch shell, past the white Busha or overseer and headed for the planting or weeding of the hill fields. In gangs of thirty or sixty men and women to a field, they sang or chanted together as they worked. The Negro Driver was ever-present with his thong and the lash fell on lagging workers.

The babies were kept nearby in field 'nurseries' or 'trays' while the toddlers were put to work pulling vines and weeds. Larger children formed the 'little gang' to collect grass for the animals, bring in the firewood, clean the cookhouse stove or the bath.

A conch shell blew for a breakfast stop, and again for a

noon dinner. The shell sounded again for a long afternoon of work until sundown. After this the women cooked supper over their outdoor cookpots while their men tended to the provision ground and animals.

Cane shoots took about 15 to 18 months to mature and ripen, during which time they had to be manured and weeded often. Ripe cane was cut each year during the spring months. Gangs of men and women worked in long rows with their sharp machetes called 'bills' flashing in the sun. The stalks were piled onto four-pronged carriers on the backs of mules or donkeys, or into a donkey cart. Little boys drove the animals and carts to the mill.

A SWEETENED ARROW. On Tortola there was one really unique way of getting cane from the higher fields on the steep hillsides down to the mill below. A V-shaped trough ran down the mountain and as one early writer described it, "this is a canal of wood that brings everything consigned to it downwards and proves an easy method of conveying produce from the hills. Cane bundles are dropped successively down this dry shoot, and taken thence by the lads, whose dexterity was shown in avoiding the loose sticks that rebound on reaching the bottom."

Another visitor wrote of nearly losing his life to a "sweetened arrow" while riding up a mountain path because "these troughs being ranged on the inclined plane, in a line as direct as possible to the works...necessarily intersect at different intervals the zig-zag paths which lead to the mountain summits. In stepping across the range at a moment of imagined security, a single cane was thrown down the trough, and came with the velocity of an arrow impelled from a bow, and having received a check in the channel of the trough, it ascended in a curved direction to the height of our head and passed within an inch of our existence. Many instances of injury to the negroes have occurred from this cause and two who had lost their leg or arm were afterward pointed out to me."

At the bottom of the chute the canes were loaded into carts and taken directly to the grinding mill. There were only a few of the big grey stone windmills on Tortola which are a familiar sight on such other islands as Ántigua or St. Croix. There is only one windmill standing on Tortola now, at Mt. Healthy on the north coast area.

Most estates had one or more animal treadmills instead, usually called mule mills although just as often worked by oxen, horses or cattle. The treadmills stood on a slight elevation so that the cane juice could run from the rollers down a trough to a big copper receiver or a mortar cistern. From this it would be released directly down into the clarifier inside the boiling house.

The scene around the mill was one of bustle and assembly-line production. Men unloaded the cane into a huge pile near the rollers or carried it on their heads to a tilted table from which it was fed into three big iron rollers. These were fastened vertically to a central grinding shaft attached at the top to one or two long poles slanting out and down to the animals. The poles were bound to the harness of the teams of oxen or mules which walked the path, thereby turning the rollers. Sometimes the mill had an elevated path with the machinery below in the center. The path and machinery had a crude pole shelter covered in palm leaf thatch. Little boys followed the teams around all day, flicking them with whips to keep them plodding. The animals were usually blindfolded.

One or two men fed the canes into the meshed rollers which often had an attachment called a 'dumb returner' that fed the canes back again into the rollers for a second crushing. An axe or hatchet stood handy to chop off the arm or leg of any worker unlucky enough to be caught in the rollers, before the whole body could be drawn in. This was much less likely to happen with the slower-moving animal mill rollers than with the powerful fast moving ones of a windmill which required a whole crew of men to halt it.

Another gang of workers stood by to carry off the *bagasse*, the ground cane refuse which went into a huge pile nearby under an open shed. The animals of the estate were allowed to feed on the sweet *bagasse* at crop time, and their coats got sleek and thick. Later, when it was well-rotted, the *bagasse* went full circle back into the holes made for manuring new cane. A field manured with *bagasse* has a peculiar sickeningly-sweet-

31

rotten smell never to be forgotten. Sugar island residents try to stay to the leeward of it.

The freshly squeezed cane juice ran through the lead trough in the mill floor to the receiver or cistern and on to the clarifier inside the boiling room. Several of these held up to 400 gallons each; here the juice was heated to just under a boil and some temper such as wood ash, vegetable alkalis or Bristol lime added. When the scum rose to the top the fire was put out and the juice stayed there about an hour while the mass of impurities collected at the top. It was then siphoned off or drawn through a cock into a trough leading to the first of the huge boiling vats called the Grand copper.

Fresh cane juice varies widely in sugar content depending on soil, rain and care of the cane. It spoils easily and should be used within an hour of squeezing for making sugar. It takes an experienced hand to boil juice down to sugar, with many tricks of timing, tempering and testing. The Chief Boiler was always one of the most coddled slaves on any estate, along with the equally essential coopers, carpenters and masons.

A sugar boiling factory looks a little like a scene from Dante's *Inferno*, with its fires, smoke, steam and bubbling cauldrons. The furnace ran the length of the bank of coppers, underneath them, and with its openings outside where it was fed by a crew of men or older boys from a shaded woodshed built against the side of the factory. The main fuel, lacking wood, was often dried cane trash.

The slightly elevated bank of big coppers was made of

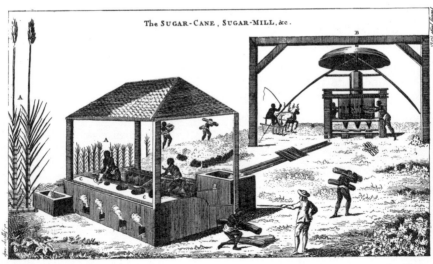

The SUGAR-CANE, SUGAR-MILL, &c.

brick or mortar with the huge vats sunk in level with its top so that a man could easily dip the boiling juice from one to another over the dividers. Overhead were the wood racks to hold the dippers and skimmers with supports for their eight-foot handles.

The juice came first into the Grand copper where it was partially boiled down as the scum was removed from time to time. These skimmings were often saved and used later in the rum process. The juice was then ladled into the Second Grand copper, boiled and skimmed further, and then dipped over into the Second Teache or third copper. Toward the end as it began to thicken it went into the small Teache or final vat.

It was up to the Chief Boiler to test and call a 'strike,' which he did by a yell or by pounding a striking iron. Helpers ran with their huge ladles and the liquid was put quickly into long wooden cooling pans where it began the crystalizing process. There were usually six of these and each cooler held one hogshead, or about 1,500 gallons of liquid. Later the grainy mass was 'potted' into hogsheads and hauled to the curing house. Here these huge barrels rested high on an open framework over a molasses cistern. Each hogshead had eight or ten holes in the bottom and into these were stuck the pithy stalks of banana or plantain leaves. The molasses drained through these stalks for about three weeks, leaving the grainy brown *muscovado* sugar inside the hogshead, now ready for use.

On the smaller islands the refining process was seldom carried further but on some of the larger ones they used to "clay" the wet brown sugar in a separate process. This involved putting a special clay on top the wet mass which was suspended in conical pots. Water was added to seep down through the clay to carry off more and more molasses until a pure, white sugar resulted.

READY FOR RUM. The molasses was not just a by-product. It was the base of rum. With a full molasses cistern each spring the planter knew he could make enough rum for estate use and have some left to barter with the North American traders. Often he sold the molasses outright to be shipped to New England where there were many rum distilleries. The income from rum or molasses often made the difference between profit or loss for the season.

The rum stillhouse was built near the molasses cistern but the copper potstills were usually located just outside. Inside the stillhouse were big wooden vats called butts which held up to 1,000 gallons of fermenting mash each. The mash might contain molasses and some water, plus some ground up *bagasse* which acted as a yeast or *mother*; skimmings from the sugar boiling and any other special flavoring the planter fancied. Some form of acid was added, usually lime, lemon, tamarind or any acid fruit. Making rum had many variations on the theme. Some planters used salt, nitre, vegetable acids or mineral acids.

A planter's fine rum, with its fragrant bouquet and just the right kick in its mellowness was often one of his many status-symbols, and the special secrets of its making were carefully kept.

When the fermented mash was ready it was drained off through a wooden trough to the copper potstill outside. This was connected by a gooseneck pipe to another big vessel called the doubler or retort. This was usually made of wood and contained low wine, a weak low-proof rum used as a starter. These two vessels were then closed and a fire started under the potstill.

As the mash cooked the steaming vapors went over into the doubler and in turn started the low-wine boiling. The combined vapors gained in proof or alcohol strength, and passed on down into the pewter 'worms.' These were hollow pipes of pewter coiled into a descending spiral shaped like a huge spring. They were suspended in a cistern of cold water. When the hot vapors ran down through the cold 'worms' they condensed—and out came rum!

Rum could also be made directly from pure cane juice without using molasses. This supposedly made the best quality rum, a clear white one which was usually aged in barrels to achieve a mellow color and taste. Some distillers lined their barrels with a white wax just to keep the rum white while it was aging. Nearly all the rum made today on Tortola is made directly from pure cane juice, but it is not always aged before reaching the consumer.

A letter writer of 1843 speaks of the scene at Brewer's Bay

on Tortola's north shore where "a vessel lay embowered in cliffs, except where seaward, the waves roll in across a sunken reef."

"All was bustle and activity, the negro-sailors were engaged in shipping hogsheads in their *moses* boat and at the works close by was a sugar mill in full operation. The manager and myself reclined in a gallery overlooking the scene... there was ample occupation for the eyes and ears... here the fire-man bellowed on his imps that supplied the fuel-trash, they call it. Then a reeking Negro came to the mill-trough to admit syrup into the copper; mules kicking; boys cracking their thongs; women chattering as they fed the cane rollers. In one corner an ox and the spare mules were consorted at their meal of cane tops; in another, you might observe an old negress by turns coaxing or angry with her sable bantlings; here the cooper plied his noisy trade, there a staid slave quietly watched the rum-mill."

"... those employed at the sugar house have a scorching task, that of removing the scum constantly rising in the coppers; at the rum-still they have cooler, though, I believe, far less healthy occupation; indeed, the sleek skin of a sugar boiler is notable here."

Apropos of that *moses* boat, old prints of the period show slaves rolling hogsheads down a beach toward a tiny dinghy sort of boat, tipped up on its side by other men, ready to cradle the huge barrel on its thwarts as the reeds did Moses. A sailing schooner waits offshore.

Not all the planters could ship their barrels out by small boat to Roadtown or a waiting schooner; most of them had to get them over the hills on narrow rocky trails. The 1843 writer tells of watching the loads come down from Windy Hill with "mules bringing sugar in tierces down the mountain for shipment. To effect this, they harness the animals by couples into shafts that bear the casks as its poles do a sedan... the drivers' incessant bawling with the beasts and themselves, together with the smacks of their thongs and the mules kicking, while their heavy burdens creaked over the tortuous descent...."

This observer had strong opinions on all he saw in Tortola and one of his comments was that "bondage here is in a poor state, rife with ignorance, and sin, and shame... but not a misery of pain and want...not ill-treated or neglected except in isolated cases."

The treatment of the slaves did vary widely as everyone knew. At crop time, for instance, on one plantation the workers might have all the fresh cane juice and molasses they could use; on another they might get the whip for taking a spare calabash full. While the work was hard all year 'round, it rose to a feverish pitch of activity during crop time, and the mill ran 24 hours a day with slaves working in three shifts.

When the annual 'Crop Over' came, it was customary to have a vacation period of wild revelry equal to Christmas festivities; with drinking, dancing and presents for all.

Slowly then the workers began the long summer routine of cleaning up the factory and the estate in general. The cooper set about next year's sugar barrels or this year's puncheons for rum. The wheelwright repaired the carts, the blacksmith made new tools and new shoes for the animals. The hogsheads of sugar were sent off to market.

If there were a windmill on the estate, one important job was to dismantle the precious sails when the grinding season was over, for storage through the hurricane months. A windmill was a temperamental thing at the best of times and even a sudden shift in the wind could send the sails running wild and out of control. A hurricane could tear apart the blades and sails.

The earlier sails of canvas had no reefing mechanism. Later, a type of louvred or slatted wood sail was introduced, plus the use of a mill roof which turned on a big horizontal roller to change sail positions. It took a crew of six or seven men to lean and push on the long beam attached to the turning roof to get the sails shifted in a high wind. It looked picturesque, but it was sometimes extremely hazardous and a careless person could be decapitated by getting too close to the whirling blades.

While the men attended to their cleanup jobs after the sugar making, the women made some of the annual supply of new clothing and did the planting in their own provision grounds.

NO SMALL AMOUNTS. The Master meanwhile went to work on his account books and on his complicated shopping list for supplies and provisions which he would send to his agent in Bristol or London along with the shipment of sugar.

Yearly, a planter might have to order as much as 1,000 yards of Osnaburg, a coarse duck or linen from which were made the trousers and shirts of the men and the outer petticoats worn by the women. Each person had a five yard allotment of this. For lighter clothing he might send for several hundred yards of calicos and madras, or some striped linsey. He bought hundreds of yards of blue bays or Pennistones, a coarse woolen cloth. Each slave had a six yard allotment of this. There would be new hats or colored caps ordered for the men. The women wore a madras headpiece twisted into a toque.

The annual order list for a medium-sized plantation would include perhaps 50,000 nails, a few thousand puncheon rivets, new cattle chains, dozens of new hoes, 25 bundles of iron hoops for barrels and twice this of wooden hoops, new ox bows and yokes, sheets of lead, new coppers, skimmers, ladles and dippers, barrels of tar and perhaps a new grindstone. Add Bristol lime for temper, dozens of cane cutting bills, bar iron for the black-smith, and new tools for the cooper, carpenter and wheelwright.

The main food imports were acquired from North American traders—the salt pork, herring in barrels, plenty of Indian corn, tierces of rice, oil, pitch, turpentine, masts and spars for boats, horses, beef, hogs and sheep. The order from England, however, would include a supply of soap, perhaps candles, hogsheads of salt, firkins of salted butter, barrels of flour, kegs of peas, jugs of groats, boxes of tobacco, small and large iron cook pots and enough coarse blankets for all.

The slaves grew many of their own provisions including the tropical fruits, yams, greens, plantains, guinea corn, peppers and cassava. They had a good supply of limes, sour oranges, guava, soursop, papaya and mango. They kept some fowl and if their sales of surplus food were good enough at Saturday market, they might invest in goats, swine or cattle for themselves.

The planter took care of medical costs for the slaves; each estate had its own hospital or sickhouse, although they were far from today's standards. The doctor rode out twice a week on his rounds from Roadtown. It paid to feed, clothe and doctor the slaves well since every non-productive person represented higher costs to the planter. Only the stupid or sadistic master treated his slaves badly.

The planter had to figure on an annual salary for his carpenter, cooper, wheelwright and blacksmith if he had no skilled slaves for the jobs. There would also be a salary for the Manager and Overseer and a bonus for the Chief Boiler. If he kept white servants he must pay them also, as the time was long past when he could count on having white slaves as in the mid-1600's in the West Indies. At that time there were nearly as many white slaves as black.

The planter also reckoned on Colonial taxes, his wharfage and storage charges in Roadtown and England, his shipping bill for sugar and for the merchandise order sent out from England. He might need to buy or barter for new mules, steers and oxen.

By the time the planter provided new clothes for himself and the family out of profits, he rarely had enough left for his wife's coveted new piano or the extra 'pipe' of Madeira wine he would like for himself.

On the larger, wealthier islands the planter might well leave all these bothersome details of buying and selling to a Manager or to his agent in England, while he and the Mistress took the long sail home to England for a round of visits, or even for a jaunt across the channel to see all the changes in Paris. But in Tortola it was the rare planter who didn't stick to his fields, factory and bookkeeping if he wanted to show enough profit to keep going and to shore up a little ahead for drought or hurricane years.

Given the right luck and hard work it could be a very satisfying life for the planter and his family in spite of all the problems of Colonial living, but it was scarcely as romantic as usually pictured. At all times it was a gamble because of the uncertainties of weather and wars. On Tortola the whole picture was complicated by uncooperative topography and isolation from the mainstream of the British West Indian life.

Above all, everything about the life was complicated for both master and slave by the evils of an economic system based on slavery.

The Friendly
Persuasion

The saga of the Quakers, the Society of Friends colony in Tortola, reveals one of the most unusual episodes in the island's history. Today the word Quaker connotes a quiet person, attendance at worship for meditation, selfless service to others and well organized social service to the world.

In the mid-17th Century, Quakers were thought of as challenging some of the established religious theories in England. They were often persecuted and some of their members were hounded out of the country. Two of them, Mary Fisher and Anne Austin, went out to Barbados in 1655 on their way to even worse troubles in New England.

Barbados became a regular stopover point for other Quakers enroute to North America. They soon had five Meeting houses on the island and the Society of Friends flourished there under an uneasy truce with island authorities. They were forbidden to teach the slaves and gradually their decline set in after several decades of success. By 1744 there were only some one hundred Quakers left on Barbados.

Slowly the Quakers spread in growing numbers throughout the islands to the north, including the British Virgins. Joshua Fielding and William Piggott came out from England together in 1726, and Fielding made his way as far north as Spanishtown on Virgin Gorda where the Governor had his headquarters. Fielding reported that there were 78 white men there and still

85 men left on Anguilla. When he reached Tortola he found about 100 men there.

The Quaker colonies on Virgin Gorda and Tortola were founded in 1727, according to a thorough little book written in 1923 by Charles F. Jenkins of Philadelphia, an historian for the Society of Friends whose book was published by the Friends Bookshop in London.

Legend, however, has the Quakers settled on Tortola much earlier, and since folk history is sometimes more interesting than official facts, it is through legend that the unconfirmed connection of the famous English Penn family with Tortola enters into the story.

William Penn, later of Pennsylvania, and his brother Richard were sons of the famous English Admiral Lord Penn. The story goes that when the two brothers joined the Society of Friends their father disowned them. The Admiral himself had, along with Army General Venables, muffed an expensive expedition against Santo Domingo and had taken Jamaica instead.

The Penn family were Royalists in the Cromwell era when Catholics were being sold into West Indian slavery and the Penn boys must have heard many West Indian tales. The young Penns knew King Charles II and were on familiar ground with the Royal Family. One story is that while the brothers incurred their father's wrath over their becoming Quakers, they incurred only the amusement of the King. William, following the Quaker custom of not taking off his hat to any temporal ruler once failed to doff his to the King. The King then violated royal custom and promptly doffed his to William. Puzzled, William asked him why he did this, to which the King replied that since it was customary for at least one gentleman on meeting another to doff his hat, he *had* to do it if William didn't.

William was often in trouble with the authorities and once when brought before a magistrate for helping to hold a banned Friend's Meeting, told the judge that he should "tremble at the words of the Lord." For this William and his followers were ridiculed and dubbed Quakers, a term which first was an insult but later became acceptable to the Friends themselves.

40

The legend goes that William and his brother supposedly tossed a coin to see which was to go to the North American continent and which to Tortola to found colonies. This bit of un-Quakerish gambling doesn't ring true. William, in any case, founded Pennsylvania to his everlasting fame, but whether brother Richard came to Tortola is still a mystery. Another version has it that the brothers secured large grants of land in the New World because the King was much in debt to the Admiral when their father died. This was the least painful form of payment.

There is little to substantiate the story about the Penns and Tortola, as officially the Quaker experiment began there much later than their time. Nothing about all the official history accounts for those myriads of persons named Penn living on the island today. They combine a gentle manner with the intelligence and astuteness worthy of William himself.

QUAKER LEADERS. There are a number of other prominent island names interwoven in the Quaker story—the Pickerings, Lettsoms, Nottinghams, Hodges, Thorntons, Callwoods, Zeagers, Clandaniels and many others.

The first prominent Quaker there was Governor John Pickering of Virgin Gorda who supposedly moved his capital over to Tortola. He, like all Friends, was a conscientious objector to fighting. He had become a Quaker while in office at a time of war, which caused a fair amount of anguish to the worried non-Quakers.

The second Governor, Capt. John Hunt, was not a Quaker and he planned to raise a great sum of money to build a chain of forts and towers for defense. He was reported a "great Enemy and Despiser of Friends." The Friends anticipated trouble after an Act of Parliament required every family in the islands to keep firearms in their homes and to respond to every alarm. They asked aid of London to bring pressure on Governor Hunt to release them from this obligation.

Governor Hunt earlier had married a Miss Nottingham. probably the daughter of the two Quakers who had arrived in 1748 from England, and who many years later freed their slaves and gave them their estate. Governor Hunt beat his wife because she insisted on going to Meeting.

At the later time in 1778, when Samuel and Mary Nottingham examined their consciences and gave their slaves not only their freedom but their Estate Long Look they complicated land titles even unto today. The freed slaves and their descendants were to have communal title in perpetuity, and their direct descendants had still the right to a plot of land there. Over the centuries the descendants multiplied and the boundaries of Estate Long Look had grown fuzzy and needed defining. So now the Government has straightened it all out equitably.

The eldest son of ex-Governor Pickering became a Quaker in England where he was schooled. He returned to Tortola several times as an enterprising sea-going trader, and here he 'married out' of the faith to the daughter of Bezaliel Hodge, wealthiest planter on the island, but remained a Quaker himself. After he died, his wife married John Purcell of Tortola who was later Governor.

DOCTOR AND POET. The most famous Friend of all this prominent group was John Coakley Lettsom, who was born in 1744 on Little Jost Van Dyke island off Tortola. He died in London in 1815, famous as a physician, writer and philanthropist.

Dr. Lettsom's undying fame rests also on his humorous masterpiece:

> I, John Lettsom
> Blisters, Bleeds and Sweats 'em.
> If, after that, they please to die,
> I, John Lettsom.

The first reference to the Lettsom family as Tortolans was made in 1732 but the family probably moved earlier from Anguilla. Edward Lettsom and his wife, Mary Coakley, who was descended from an Irish Baronet, lived on Little Jost Van Dyke, even then one of the lonesomest spots in this area. They grew cotton there with the help of 50 slaves. Edward also had a sugar cane plantation across the channel at Cane Garden Bay on Tortola's north shore.

The most remarkable thing about this couple is that they had seven sets of male twins, of which the famous Doctor John was half of the final set. All of the first six sets died.

Doctor John Lettsom packed a good deal of living into his 71 years. About age five he was sent to England for schooling. The parents kept his twin brother Edward at home. After the elder Lettsom died, John came out from London in 1767, already trained in medicine, to settle his share of the family estate. He found the island pulling out of a slump after some bad years, and reckoned that his slaves were worth from £60 to £100 each. As their worth was totaled at £444, he could not have inherited too many.

Dr. Lettsom found his mother remarried to a cooper. He felt free to exercise his Quaker conscience and he gave his slaves their freedom, becoming as he termed it a "voluntary beggar." His Quaker love of plainness in dress and way of life made him critical of the Tortolan way where "everything is splendor, dress, shew, equipage, everything that can create an opinion of their importance is exerted to the utmost of their credit."

Even by this time, the main Quaker movement had died out on Tortola, and Dr. Lettsom's close older friend ex-Governor Pickering died the year after his arrival. Later the doctor was to name his own son Pickering Lettsom in his memory.

Lettsom's impecunious state didn't last long. He set himself up in medical practice and made near £2,000 in six months. Without competition, he had a clientele of the entire population: 1,200 white settlers and nearly 10,000 slaves. He often, he said, saw 50 to 100 patients before breakfast. This was no mean accomplishment, even allowing for the island custom of breakfasting at eleven. The afternoons he spent in rounds of the plantations, made by mule back or trading sloop.

Dr. Lettsom decided to return to London once he had saved £2,000. When he gave half of his savings to his mother, one friend termed it "quixotic" of him.

Back in London he became an active Quaker and was the signer of many of the Annual Letters of the Society sent out to Tortola. His interest continued to the end, as he signed the final Letter sent out to Tortola marking the end of Quaker activity on the island in the mid-1780's.

The energy and ability which made Lettsom so popular on Tortola won him much recognition also in London. He founded the London Medical Society, wrote a book or two, set up a Sea Bathing House at Margate for medical purposes, founded the Royal Humane Society and jumped into the middle of the raging controversy over vaccination, which he favored.

Lettsom became a close friend of Benjamin Franklin and many other prominent North Americans, who were also friends of another Tortolan Quaker, William Thornton, then living in Philadelphia.

A somewhat ironical thing happened to the good doctor shortly before his death. His son, Pickering Lettsom, had gone out to Tortola to practice law and had married an enormously wealthy widow. She had inherited some 1,000 slaves from her own grandfather, Bezaliel Hodge, whose daughter had married Governor Pickering's eldest son.

Pickering Lettsom's new wife was sixteen years older than he, but he died about a month after the marriage, She died some two months later of the proverbial broken heart, and left her whole fortune to her new father-in-law.

So, the good Quaker, Dr. Lettsom in London who had freed his own slaves when he was a young man, found himself as an old man the reluctant owner of 1,000 slaves! He died before he could decide what to do about this inheritance. The entire estate went to a grandson of his, who then became worth £10,000 annually. Shortly before the doctor's death in 1815 he declared he was the only surviving West Indian Quaker.

THE FAMOUS THORNTON. One of Dr. Lettsom's closest friends when they were young Quaker gentlemen was William Thornton

44

who was to become equally famous. Thornton, too, had inherited slaves on Tortola at the time he was in London studying medicine and working in the Quaker movement.

Thornton went later to live in Philadelphia and about this time conceived the plan of freeing his 70 island slaves and moving with them to establish a colony in Sierra Leone in Africa. Thornton had a low opinion of the climate of his birthplace, Tortola, and said it was hotter than Africa and less healthful.

The young man proposed to use his fortune to do this and to include many ex-slaves from North America. His plan was one among many proposed and there were actually several colonies of this kind set up in Sierra Leone which for one reason or another all failed.

Much as Dr. Lettsom wanted to see freedom for all slaves, he had advised his friend and fellow Quaker not to engage in one of the African colonizing projects, but to return to Tortola and make himself really independent there.

To the lasting benefit of the new United States, Thornton went neither to Africa nor Tortola at that time. He stayed right on in Philadelphia practicing medicine, and as an amateur archi-

tect designed the winning building in a competition for the city Library which Benjamin Franklin had founded.

When young Thornton married he took his wife on a wedding trip to Tortola where he decided to stay and practice medicine while settling up his family estate. At the same time he petitioned the local Council and Legislature for permission to free his slaves.

In March of 1792, Secretary of State Thomas Jefferson put an advertisement in the North American newspapers asking for competitive architectural plans for the Capitol building and the President's house, later the White House, to be built in the new City of Washington.

Dr. Thornton in Tortola heard of the competition and wrote asking permission to enter it. Meanwhile he went to work on a set of plans for the Capitol and after some months sailed for the States with them. He found the competition closed. However, in showing his designs to his friend George Washington at the Philadelphia capital, he discovered that the Commissioners of the District of Columbia had not been satisfied with any of the other entries. President Washington sent Thornton off with a letter to the Commissioners.

Thornton's plans for the Capitol were accepted, which just might prove that distance, talent and knowing the right people were no handicap. He collected the award, a lot in the new City of Washington valued at £100 plus $500 in gold. In addition, he later became one of the three Commissioners for building the new city. Later, when Jefferson was designing the beautiful Georgian buildings for his new University of Virginia he asked Thornton's help.

Thornton's Quaker principle of non-violence was put to the test when the British burned Washington during the War of 1812. He joined the militia and fought to save his Capitol building and the city. He also was noted for his race track and stable of good horses on his Maryland farm. And finally, he was not adverse in these years to owning slaves, as there is a bill of sale for two he acquired from John C. Calhoun.

The old Thornton estate on Tortola lies at Pleasant Valley just off the West End road, and had an imposing Greathouse on it. When he died, he owned a half share along with his brother. His total estate was valued at nearly $70,000, including half of the 120 slaves at Pleasant Valley. He had reckoned his part of the income from it as £3,000 annually.

There was another Tortola Quaker who became rich and famous in Philadelphia. He was Richard Humphreys, who made his fortune as a goldsmith and left $10,000 of it to found a school in that city to teach trades to the descendants of slaves. It has become a fine Normal School under the State system, but its funds are still managed by members of the Philadelphia Quakers Yearly Meeting.

There was always a strong link between the Pennsylvania and Tortola Quakers and many visitors came down to the island from the British North American colonies in the earlier days of the movement. Among them were Thomas Chalkley, John Cadwallader and John Estaugh, all of whom died suddenly from one of the island's deadly fevers. They were buried in the Quaker graveyard at Fat Hog Bay not far from the Meeting House. Chalkley in 1741 had written a series of rather sad letters to his wife in which he revealed some of the tribulations of the Friends, in particular those of one of the high-spirited young ladies of the group.

THE DETERMINED CREATURE. "The Dear Young Creature, whose Father had turned her Out of Doors for coming to Friends Meeting, Say [said], had he been at all that Charge to buy her fine Cloaths, & taught her to Sing, & Dance, & all for nothing?"

"I understand from the Governour, That the General Hath sent for the Warlike arms here, Saying If the People were Quakers they would have no need for them, that He should want them at Antigua. . . . he has still Continued Friend Pickering, Governour of the Island, to the mortification of all the great swordsmen."

'The Governour's wife, her two Sisters, Capt. Hunt's Wife, and the young Woman whose Father turn'd her Out of Doors, wore Hoops before they were Convinced of the principles of our Friends, being thoroughly convinced they could wear them no longer and Divers fine young people have left them off since."

THE VIRGIN

Freebooters Pt.

or N.E. Point

Treasurer

Prickly I.

Moskitos

Cammanoes

Little Van Dykes

Jost
Van Dykes

Guana

Scrubb I.

Dog I.

Green I.

Brass I.

St James's

orango

TORTOLA

Sunk
Rock

E.

Beef I.

or Serpents I.
Green I.

St THOMAS

Town

Thatch
I.

Drake's Bay
from 16 to 25
Fathom

Broken
City

Round

St Ginger

Dan.

Savanna

Frenchman's Kd.

Little
Passage I.

Buck
I.

Cun

Salt I.

Little Saba

Carvel I.

St JOHNS

Castle

Witch

Peters

Dead
Chest

Coopers

ge I.

Dan.

Normands

or Crab I.

Crawl Bay

Barp

Medic

at Harbour

Birds Key or Round I.

Salt River Bay

Debouquement des Vierges or
Southern Channel

Hams Bluff

Christianstaed

Fridrichstaed

Green
Key

Bocken I.

Sand Point

Breids Pt.

Watch house Pt.

East Point
and Reef

St CROIX
or Santa Cruz

Lime tree Bay

Dan.

ISLANDS

a Hat I. E.

Dangerous Reef

Sink Rock

Drake's Channel

ricker

Sombrero
or Hat I.

10

8

N GORDA or
nish Town E.

7

Passage I.

6

5

Salt
Pond

Anguilla E

the Channel

St Martins

Channel

THE

nch

Dutch
Salt Pond

LEEWARD

10

Town of Diep

St CHRIST

Mt Miser

vulgo St

Saba D.

10

St Eustatia D.

Sandy Point Town

Charles Fort

Old Road Town

Basse terre Town

30

15

10

10

Nags Head

the Narrows

Charles Town

y Ground

Dorcas Powell, the Dear Young Creature who was put Out of Doors, had married at 15 and was widowed at 18. After her father turned her out she was permitted to visit him when he was ill, and at his bedside met the clergyman whom the non-Quakers had imported to combat the Quaker influence. Her father made it a condition of reconciliation that she marry this clergyman, which she did. She told the Quaker committee considering her case that she wished to remain a Friend but "had got a very good husband and should go with much freedom to his worship." She did, and the Quakers 'read her out' of Meeting. Later, after her clergyman husband had died, she moved to St. Croix and there married a third time. She converted her new husband to the Friends' faith and together they established a Meeting there, which didn't last too long. When next heard of Dorcas had gotten herself into trouble with the Philadelphia Meeting by holding unauthorized meetings on a visit there.

The rise and decline of the Quaker colony at Fat Hog Bay spanned a time of only about 45 years from 1727 until the Monthly Meeting was abandoned in 1762. A few members continued to meet for worship in Roadtown until the time of the final Letter sent out from London by Dr. Lettsom in 1780. This was the end of the official correspondence. A few years later another of those travelling Philadelphians gathered up the records of the group at Tortola and took them back for safe-keeping to the City of Brotherly Love where they remain today in a strongbox.

During the 1830s and 40s at the peak of the anti-slavery movement which was strongly supported by the Quakers everywhere, a number of Friends came to Tortola to report on conditions there. Among them were the famous Joseph John Gurney, George Truman, John Jackson and Thomas Longstreth, all of whom wrote copiously on the subject.

Then, no more of the Friends from Philadelphia visited Tortola until in 1913 their historian, Charles Jenkins, came to take a final look at the crumbled remnants of the graveyard at Fat Hog Bay. He was able to unravel the story of this small band of Friends who played such an influential part in history in London, Philadelphia, Washington and Tortola.

Century of Turmoil

The Napoleonic Wars inaugurated a new era for the British Virgins. It was a time of great change; first came the abolition of the slave trade, then the freeing of the slaves, followed by local insurrections. There were international wars going on, both large and small. It was a lively time during the first part of the century; after this a general economic decline set in from which the British Virgin Islands are just now recovering.

In 1801, Tortola became a rendezvous for the British naval ships which cruised the Mona Passage in search of foreign prize ships or used the Roadtown harbour as a staging area for attacking other islands. That year, the naval Commandant of the British Leewards, Sir Alexander Cochrane sent Rear-Admiral Duckworth of *The Leviathan* out from Tortola with his squadron to capture St. Thomas and St. Croix. This they did rather neatly without firing a shot, using instead a fancy exchange of letters with the two Danish Governors pointing out their gun power and overwhelming numbers of men.

The English planters, who formed the majority on the Danish islands, welcomed the change from stiff Danish trade restrictions, but the British Virgin residents probably had some reservations about it as this meant a temporary end of the profitable smuggling in and out of St. Thomas.

The English held these Danish islands only a few months this first time, but they returned in 1807 to retake them without firing a shot. The Danish Governors were again allowed to send an inspection party to the English fleet to establish that they were overwhelmed in numbers, so the Danes could capitulate with honor. This time the English held the two islands for seven years.

An English naval surgeon, John Waller, writes of the capture of Spanish and French prize ships near the Mona Passage, and of taking them into St. Thomas to dispose of them. A Lieutenant was sent off to Tortola with the ships' papers to get the prizes condemned, as there was no English Vice-Admiralty Court on St. Thomas. Meanwhile the temporary English Governor McLean gave a ball that night at St. Thomas on the King's Birthday.

Later, Surgeon Waller was back again at Tortola, this time to join a convoy of ships for England. Since the Roadtown harbour could hold up to 400 ships at a time, as one eyewitness pointed out, it was used to rendezvous merchant ships for the voyage home. Waller termed Tortola "one of the least interesting of the Leeward Islands ... high and barren mountains ... exhibit a black and bleak appearance. The water was gloomy and stormy, and the dark rocks around reminded me of the coast of Norway. The town, like most of the English towns in the torrid regions, was ill-built, and presented no object of interest. But, if the exterior of the houses exhibited nothing very inviting, within at least hospitality presided in a very extensive degree. The convoy being assembled, the 'merchants' were all converted into taverns, where no introduction was required, nor any reckoning thought of. I observed here a singular example of this virtue, which I was told was perpetual—a huge bowl of punch, holding two or three gallons, standing all the forenoon upon the side-board, with a number of tumblers about it, and several ladles; and whoever is thirsty has only to walk in and help himself."

Surgeon Waller didn't sail off with his convoy, not due to too much rum punch, but because he was ordered suddenly to the recently-captured little French island of Marie-Galante, where, as he remarked gloomily, the last four medical officers and over half the garrison had died, and the other half was in hospital. By contrast, Tortola must have seemed quite a healthy island.

About this time, Tortola was still exporting a goodly amount of sugar, some 2,500 hogsheads annually, but the effect of the war with the French is shown by a drop of about one-third in the output since the turn of the century. There were then 1,300 white persons in Tortola, 220 persons of color and 9,000 slaves.

The Methodists now had their booming membership up to 2,010 of the slaves. There were also 30 white members, but later the ruling white group was to accuse the Methodists of generally stirring up trouble by Christianizing the slaves.

A SLAVER'S ACCOUNT. The abolition of the Slave Trade in 1807 came without any surprise to the West Indies since it had been argued bitterly for years in England, with mounting pressures for the measure. One of the last cargoes of slaves sold on Tortola has a fascinating story behind it, told by another seagoing surgeon whose name was Jerrard John Howard. He not only sailed to Guinea in Africa and to the West Indies, but also translated Ovid's *Metamorphosis* in his spare time.

Howard recounts that the *General Abercrombie* was coming up from Trinidad to the Virgins in 1803 when it was wrecked off St. Croix on little Buck Island a former privateer's hangout. Ninety slaves were sent into the Danish town of Christiansted by jolly boats. They were promptly seized at the Fort and detained as being smuggled. Meanwhile, the sailors left aboard the floundered ship on the reef got drunk and the rest of the slaves were put off on Buck Island.

Finally, all the Negroes were released by the Danes and taken to Tortola, where they could not be sold because the ship was under British colors, and they could not be landed under Danish colors either. This was handled neatly by calling it a 'shipwreck' and the slaves were sold at auction. The agent of the shipping line bought them to resell for the Company which had sent them there. Writer Howard grumbled that he had to wait for the sales for his salary. He also said bluntly "Tortola is well nigh the most miserable, worst-inhabited spot in all the British possessions ... even this unhealthy part of the globe appears overstocked with each description of people except honest ones."

Howard probably was aiming his complaint at the company agent, as quite an argument over salvage claims and salaries had ensued, and there was talk of appealing the whole issue to the High Court of Denmark. He was also annoyed that while Tortola was supposed to have 11,000 inhabitants it had only 13 white women. Worse, he said, the average man, "works all day, real or pretended; five o'clock he eats, then three hours of drinking, then cards, dice; late at night he sleeps it off."

The disgruntled surgeon went back and forth to St. Croix in search of a neutral passage home via Copenhagen. He must have returned later to Tortola, possibly with a bride along or to marry one of the local 13, as his widow was reported still alive on Tortola in the late 1830's and in possession of his *Notes On A Slaving Voyage.*

THE HODGE AFFAIR. Tortola was already in a sorry state when a totally unexpected and terrible thing happened. A wealthy planter, Arthur William Hodge, Esq. of Estate Bellevue, was tried for murdering one of his slaves, Prosper, after the slave let a mango fall from a tree he was posted to watch.

There was not much doubt that Hodge was guilty. He was notoriously sadistic to his slaves as various witnesses brought

out vividly during the trial. Hodge was a member of the local Council, a so-called Liberal, with a good education, polished manners and influential friends in England.

The court case rocked the whole of the West Indies and England, as well as turning Tortola itself into a churning, seething sea of violent opinions. The case symbolized changing attitudes toward slavery and the treatment of Negroes. While the majority of slave owners were not at all like Hodge, there was still a time lag between the islands, where slavery was believed an economic necessity by the plantation owners, and England where the liberals were thinking in more humanistic terms. The case brought the whole issue of slavery to a head.

Actually, no one on Tortola of either race really believed Hodge would be hanged, as his defense was based on a legal fundamental; his claim that slaves were private property and that he had a right to do as he pleased with them, including severe punishment resulting in death. The English sense of justice denied this concept; true, a slave was property, but he was first of all a man, and to all men under the Union flag the laws of Great Britain offered protection against cruelty.

To everyone's shock, Hodge was declared guilty of murder and was hanged behind the jail in Roadtown. His body made the journey to the white cemetery across the bay from Roadtown in the customary long line of funeral boats. Prosper lay in the slaves' graveyard which ironically was located just below Hodge's beautiful Estate.

A postscript to this is recorded by a visitor who came to Tortola after the slaves were freed. He speaks in 1840 of a canebrake fire which broke out in the fields of a Mr. Hodge, son of "the unfortunate man who had been connected with some powerful families in England, but nevertheless was executed for the murder of a slave."

"It is said," he reports "that the authorities in Tortola would have passed over this offense, but a report of the case reached England and produced so much excitement that a positive order was issued directing his prosecution ... during this fire my friend mentioned to me that this plantation had often been on fire ... the relation of the melancholy fate of the father and the repeated afflictions of the son, cast me into a sad train of thought—as if the hand of God was seen even now—scourging with the fire the spot upon which these cruelties had been inflicted on the helpless slaves."

After Hodges' trial and death, the relationship between the races was never quite the same again, although it would be nearly a quarter century yet before the slaves were finally freed.

TROUBLED TIMES. All of the West Indian islands were beset by creeping economic decline, the outcome of prolonged wars, disrupted markets and many periods of drought early in the century. A Tortola visitor reported that in 1815 scarcely one-fifth of the island was in cultivation.

The Virgins, however, along with St. Kitts, Nevis and Anguilla were made into the long-sought separate Leeward Island Colony in 1816. The planters were hopeful of good years ahead, but hope faded after a severe hurricane swept the islands in 1819 destroying much of Roadtown. Another of those eyewitness visitors said that every estate was damaged and that on some not a single hut or single cane of sugar was left standing. Altogether it was the worst hurricane in the recollection of the oldest inhabitants. Earlier reporters made the same remark concerning the devastating one of 1772, but in truth all hurricanes were disastrous to plantation owners.

Storms were not the only source of turmoil. The basic questions of the rights of man raised by the Hodge trial and by the earlier Quaker attitudes were coming to a crisis, not only in the islands but throughout the civilized world. On Tortola, the uncertainty felt by both slaves and owners made the times difficult for everyone. The slaves were impatient for freedom. The planters were yearly deeper in debt and convinced that freedom for the slaves meant the doom of their whole shaky economy. They expected to have to abandon their investments and leave the island. Many estates were sold; many went for unpaid taxes, and absentee ownership grew each year. So many owners left for England or the new United States that a special class of attorney-agent sprang up.

Mortgages prevailed and when the hurricanes struck, the

owners or agents found themselves without resources to rebuild the sugar and rum works. Sugar, rum and molasses—once the foundation of fortunes—had become gradually the commitment from which it was difficult to escape without great losses. The hardier planters took their losses and decided to hang on.

The greatest blow to the planters' security came with the discovery of a slave plot in 1831, just three years before Emancipation. The plot was simple; murder all the white males, plunder the island, seize the ships, and sail off to Haiti with all the wives and daughters of their former masters.

According to the St. Thomas historian John Knox, when the plan was discovered, a messenger went off post-haste to St. Thomas with a plea for help. Danish Commander Rhode sent a Man-o'-War brig, the *St. Jan*, which arrived at noon on September 11th and stayed by for more than a week until the planters' fears had subsided.

The islanders had sent also to St. Kitts for help, but got 'no sympathy or aid . . . and the officers of government and the inhabitants felt doubly grateful to Commander Rhode and the Captain of the brig. . . ."

More white persons than ever left Tortola and the outer islands after this scare, until less than 500 remained, or approximately half of the former residents.

EMANCIPATION. Freedom came to the islands' 9,000 Negroes in 1834. Its effect on Tortola depended on whose viewpoint was being expressed. The planters received only £72,940 in compensation from the British government. An official report in 1798 had valued these slaves at £40 each, or some £360,000. The value of property and of slaves had declined in the interim, but the planters claimed they were grossly under-compensated.

The freed Negroes generally stayed on the plantations, often on the same one. They were now paid 6d a day for holing and other field work; a cottage was supplied free, also provision grounds and pasture were rent free. The status-quo remained much the same except for the Negro's growing sense of dignity, the worth of his labor and his freedom to change masters. The planters found it expeditious to continue many of the old services

free, such as providing clothing and medical care, if they wished to hold their good workers.

A few years later when the three visiting Quakers were down from Philadelphia checking up on the effects of freedom they reported that "slavery went off without one single incident of tumult or disturbance." They found that the non-slaves at Thornton's old Pleasant Valley Estate worked fast, earnestly and cheerfully, in contrast to those still slaves they saw on other islands. They noted 53 children in a nearby plantation school, and said that the ex-slaves were paid 12½ cents per day by then with rent free house and garden. They could keep cows, swine, poultry and goats.

The planters, however, were grumbling that their free workers were paid more per day than similar workers in England and weren't putting in equal effort.

The visiting Quakers also rode out to Long Look, the old Nottingham estate given to their freed slaves in 1798, to check up on how these inheritors were making out. They found the land still supporting 80 persons in 16 families, although things had been badly damaged by the severe hurricane of 1838, which had also devastated Roadtown.

They located the neglected graves at Fat Hog Bay where one hundred years before the other famous visiting Quakers were buried.

The Friends also took a look at Estate Albion and reported the owner much happier since the slaves were freed. He said the men worked better with wages as a stimulation, and he had put previously idle land back into cultivation.

THE KINGSTON EXPERIMENT. The visitors checked on Kingston, a settlement of freed Negroes also called The African Location about three miles east of Roadtown. This colony had been set up long before Emancipation after much discussion over whether slaves taken from foreign prize ships should be sent back to Africa or given their freedom locally. The King had helped establish the settlement with a grant of 160 acres of Crown Land for some 500 of these freed Negroes.

The Quakers said the Kingston group did well in good seasons and terribly in bad ones. They fished for a living and were the chief suppliers of lime for Tortola and other islands. They had made a number of lime kilns "formed of layers of wood about a foot thick and from 15 to 20 feet in diameter, alternating with layers of coral to a height of eight or ten feet." This whole structure was burned and left a residue of good building lime. To get the coral they spent hours weekly diving offshore.

In total disagreement with the Quakers was the Hon. Member of the Tortola Assembly from Jost Van Dyke island who declared "would sir that we could report their settlement in all the happiness philanthropy would shower upon them ... free, indeed, but free only to all the indolence and apathy to which a tropical climate so fatally affords ... liberty came upon them unprepared."

Opinions about Kingston varied widely with each man to his own bias, and James Smith, whose sympathies always lay with the upper dog, visited the group in 1840. He says "These people are Episcopalians, and the Rev. Mr. Alexander Botts officiates as their rector. They are a poor people and live from hand to mouth. They go to the city of St. Thomas as servants, pick up a little money, return home and remain idle until it is spent."

Joseph John Gurney, the famous Quaker who wrote his *Familiar Letters To Henry Clay of Kentucky* from the West Indies said of Kingston "We had heard reports of their poverty and idleness, but these were belied by their decent and respectable appearance. A Church is now in course of building for their use, under the order of the Bishop of Barbadoes; and a school has already formed for the education of their children."

"About 300 of them assembled, under the shade of a large Tamarind tree, and it has seldom fallen to my lot to address a more feeling, or apparently more intelligent, congregation. One thing is clear and unquestionable—that the African mind is abundantly susceptible of instruction in the great doctrines and principles of the Christian religion."

HARD TIMES. Gurney's evaluation of the general situation on the island was that "the present condition of the planters in Tortola is not very favorable, from long continued droughts, and a consequent short crop." He speaks of the migration to Trinidad, but adds that the "laborers of Tortola appeared to us to be in a condition of considerable ease and comfort." He tells of examining the accounts of two Estates and finding that the agent for the owner employed 253 Negroes and "was decidedly saving money by the substitution of free labor on moderate wages, for the deadweight of slavery."

On the other hand, James Smith declared "the condition of the colored people in this island is very degraded. They are free; it is true; but they are poor and indolent. Betting is a very common employment. I rarely walked out that I was not asked for charity. They are, however, very moderate in their demands; in general they want a 'dog,' [about two cents]. Everything on this island seems on the decline; the laborers are embarking for Trinidad where it is understood they can get good wages. I was informed that the sugar raised this year, on this island, would not pay the expense of cultivation, and that, in all probability, the island would be abandoned by the planters in five years. I hardly met with an individual who was not disposed to remove to the United States."

All these visiting writers interpreted the situation to fit their own ideas or what they had hoped to find, but they were unanimous on one thing—their protests about the difficulty of getting around. Smith puts it succinctly, "There is no carriage

60

on the island. The inhabitants travel principally on mules; there are few good horses. There are no level roads. The narrow, rough paths over and about the mountains are almost impassable, even for mules."

The Negroes, when possible, were doing their travelling right off the island as both Smith and Gurney indicated. Special schooners, known as Blackbird Hunters, had been cruising the Caribbean ever since Emancipation, transplanting freed Negroes from the smaller, poorer islands to the larger ones, but especially to Trinidad where the need for labor was insatiable.

One reason for escaping the British Virgins might well have been the "vexatious taxes" of ten shilling a year on all provision grounds or gardens not connected with an estate. This was an effective way of tying down each Negro family to living and working on an estate if they wanted land for their own use.

There were other ways of scraping by for both the whites and the ex-slaves who chose to remain. An anonymous writer alludes to the old custom of smuggling which had resumed gradually with St. Thomas and St. Croix after these islands were again Danish.

"Customs imports (at Tortola) were at a minimum ... a few shingles and deal-ends or one-half cargo of some Yankee in distress ... a few bales and crate goods ... but there can be seen in town, tea, wine, brandy, cigars, Leghorn hats and wefts and Nankings, foreign stationery, waistcoats and hoses of French silk, shirts of German linens, broges of Kentucky leather ..."

The 'good old days' weren't quite gone; only two years earlier, *HMS Speedwell* had put into Beef Island in futile search of a former associate of Captain Kidd. If the renegade Mr. Hamm was there he was deep in the 'bush' or perhaps deep underground in a pirate's grave. Beef at that time had only 38 residents but how many of them were gainfully employed in smuggling is not revealed.

Osborne's *Guide To The West Indies* notes that in 1840 there were 600 ships from all the British West Indies entering St. Thomas, while only 217 ships came there from the United States and 321 from Denmark. We can assume that of the 600 West Indian ships visiting the Danish free-port most of them were local trading sloops or schooners and that not a few carried contraband goods or brought some back home with them.

The Royal Steam Packet Company of London sponsored Osborne's early travel book and in it he tells travellers what to expect in the islands. Concerning Tortola, he reported that domestics earned one pound per month; salt cost 1 shilling per barrel; the V.I. imports were 10,964 lbs. and exports 12,966 lbs. Passengers, he said, should bring Bristol gold and silver, or Spanish dollars (worth eight shillings, three pence) or Spanish doubloons (worth seven pounds, twelve shillings).

The implications of pleasant living, involving doubloons and French silk waistcoats were merely the trappings. Times were bad and the living was hard. It was hard for the planters and harder still for the free Negroes who found freedom did not bring all they had hoped for.

A BLOW FOR ACTION. The conch shell, which for so many generations had called the slave to labor, now called the ex-slave to a new freedom. In a few short hours the island was transformed by insurrection. It all began in 1853 shortly after a cattle tax had been imposed and after a white man injured a Negro. The revolt began in Roadtown and spread all over Tortola, Beef and other nearby islands. Some of the Greathouses were emptied, burned to the ground when possible, the cane fields burned, the sugar works demolished. In panic, all the white persons who could, escaped the island.

Tortola was finished. True, there was a punitive expedition from other British islands; a Man-o'-War came and the Negroes, now truly free, took to the 'bush.' The remaining whites left for other British islands. Nothing there was now worth either the planters' or His Majesty's trouble.

Tortola went 'back to de bush,' and there it stayed for many sleepy somnambulant decades. This was the way the ex-slaves wanted it and this was the way they kept it, partly on purpose to discourage their former masters from returning. It took several new generations and a new breed of white men to help the island recover.

There remained, of course, a token form of government,

administered from one of the Leeward Islands, with officials coming now and then to the Virgins. In 1867 there was a realistic change in the old system, substituting a Legislative Council for the Assembly and Courts. The old Virgin Islands Constitution, coveted for so long before it was secured by the planters, was also dropped. Five years later these islands were placed under the Federation of Leeward Islands, the whole administered as a Crown Colony.

Gradually the long haul upward began again; this time with some other changes made. The most effective improvement was a fundamental and necessary one; the Negroes began to be given a chance to participate in their own local affairs, and to rise to the opportunities offered to them. Today they serve in every top bracket of the local government which has worked out a systematic educational system, rewarding the graduates with good jobs.

All this was achieved slowly over some fifty years of trial and error while the islands themselves seemed to slumber. In 1893 there were only two white inhabitants in Tortola—the local deputy Governor and the doctor. Thirty-eight years later, in 1931, the white population had leapt to fifteen.

The one visitor who bothered to come to Tortola during this period and write about it was a Mr. Ober searching for material to display at the World's Columbian Exposition. He described it as forsaken, and said all he found of value were two ancient cannon and some peculiar coins once in use there, which he sent up to Chicago.

The Governor, Mr. Ober said, had a 'corner' on the market in collecting these rare coins, which were made with a rude Tortolan counter-stamp over coinage of foreign nations at the time of the American Revolution when money had been so scarce in the islands.

Aside from this, almost no eye-witness came to recount anything about the closing decades of a century which had begun with such turbulence. The few scanty reports lie buried in government files. There was just nothing much to write about and no more curious travellers who felt impelled to weigh and assess the situation. The century slipped into history with a sigh.

63

Tortola &
the 20th Century

It is doubtful whether anyone noticed the Twentieth Century opening in the British Virgin Islands, but the first year brought the initial rays of hope. The islands were desperately poor, the land had gone 'back to bush,' and nobody cared too much except a few officials stationed on other islands, but still responsible for the Virgins. The home government in England had much larger problems in the Empire. The tiny cluster of the Virgins were only specks on the map.

Symbolically, though, the rejuvenation began in 1900 when the Government set up an Agricultural Experiment Station. This was a big step forward for Tortola. It meant, too, that somewhere, someone had remembered the island and was trying to help. So with the Station, hope was born; new ideas, new crops might change a dormant way of life.

Eleven years after the Experiment Station was set up, it processed 52,000 lbs. of cotton in one year at the gin built there. In addition, there was also a cane mill and sugar factory going. Plans were afoot to establish a lime industry and to get coconut groves planted.

Many governmental changes were made in the first part of the century. The Legislative Council was abolished in 1902 and the Governor-in-Council became the sole legislative authority. This form of government was to last until 1950, when a Presidential Legislature for the islands was re-established, with some members appointed and some elected.

A few years later the Leeward Island Colony was de-federated and the separated Virgin Islands area set up with its own Presidency. Then on December 31st, 1959, the Office of the Governor of the Leewards was abolished and the Administrator on Tortola became the Queen's Representative. Tortola and its dependencies are now considered a Territory.

The frequent changes in the system reflect in many ways not just a rapidly-changing world in the West Indies, but the amazing British ability to be flexible in the midst of the breakup all over the world of the Colonial system. The islanders themselves long ago learned to roll with the political punches no matter how they were governed.

The severe hurricane of 1916 gave the islands quite an economic setback, and eight years was scarcely enough recovery time before one struck again in 1924.

Tortola's main industry was livestock then, but today this is eclipsed by a burgeoning tourist industry with emphasis on yacht chartering.

The principal way of bringing in new money and of raising the standard of living during the past half century has been by migration to work outside the Colony. Tortolans haven't needed to migrate far; in an hour and a half on their fast sea-going ferries they can be in St. Thomas, 15 miles to the southwest. Here ambitious Tortolans, noted for their hard work, honesty and dignity, have been much in demand. The British island economy is strongly tied to the U.S. Virgins and Puerto Rico. The U.S. dollar is legal tender on these British islands and even the B.V.I. stamps are printed in U.S. denominations.

St. Thomas and Tortola have always had a natural affinity of geographical closeness and mutual need ever since their smuggling days; obviously things would have been simpler for both the United States islands and British Virgins if they had been under one flag all these centuries. However, who is to decide which flag? Now and then there is some half-hearted agitation on Tortola for the British islands to join those of the United States, but the age-old loyalty to Britain prevails. Emotionally

Tortolans seem against such a change even if it might make common sense. No doubt there are just as many Americans who would prefer to see Tortola develop a more equitable economy on its own without losing its uniquely British charm.

Present government policy seems to endorse this last view since the aim is to achieve complete economic independence from British government financial aid, at last making the British Virgin Islands a viable and vigorous entity with no loss to its unique mixture of "Britishness" and colourful Caribbean ambience.

One of the best things to do in Tortola is nothing. If you have unwound enough to do this, then haul yourself together again and gradually you will find there is much more to 'do' than first meets the eye. The point is to do it unhurriedly. These islands appeal to those who want to slow down, to change rhythm, to be renewed by nature a little.

Obviously the best thing to see is the magnificent scenery. It is incomparable in some areas and beautiful almost everywhere one looks. The simplest way to get around is to rent a car by the day; just amble along all the main roads you see and even some of the detours on the island without hurrying. You can do it nicely in a day. Tortola is only some twelve miles long by three miles at the widest, but most of this three in width is uphill and down again.

Some of the old scalp-raising roads have been paved recently and today's tourist is spared the unbelievable jolts, bumps and hairpin turns of just a few years back. It is still preferable to go in a four-wheel drive vehicle on some particular trips, just for one's peace of mind about the steep grades.

STILL DISTILLING. There is one active local industry which hasn't changed much in 300 years. That is the making of rum. On the other hand the making of sugar or the growing of cotton has almost ceased. The interested visitor can watch the whole old time rum process at one of the three or four local distilleries during the spring season.

The cane is still cut in the old way by hand and hauled to the little outdoor mill by cart or mule back; now and then carried

66

by truck where the location of the cane fields permit. The circular animal mill around which the mules or oxen wearily plodded no longer exists. Today a little put-put engine chugs along all day turning the rollers which are still hand-fed with cane stalks. The mules still carry off the *bagasse* to a huge pile where the other animals feast on sweet stalks.

The juice flows from the rollers into a cement cistern and then straight into the big coppers for boiling just as it did back in the 1700s. The men stoke the furnaces with cane trash; others stand before the coppers wielding huge dippers and skimmers between the boiling vats. Using this primitive system a small cane mill and boiling room can handle at least 700 gallons of juice a day.

The thick juice is often allowed to lie still overnight for cooling before 'yesterday's boil' is put into open barrels, using a big clean can for a dipper. Here it sits for some 8 to 15 days bubbling quietly until it quits 'working' and is 'dead.' No liquor will distill until it is 'dead.' It is then ready to use in making rum.

When the juice is ready, some pure spring water is brought down the hill in long oblong tin cans fitted onto a special rack on a mule's back. This water and some white lime temper is added, unless the maker has preferred to put it in during the boiling process. This is also the moment to add any other ingredients to improve the flavor in the mash.

At the time the juice is being readied for rum-making, some of the pure boiled juice is put in a large stone jug to stand a month. Then the distiller has his supply of vinegar made for the year.

The mash is put into the big copper potstills which stand elevated outside the boiling house. The fire is started under them and the whole distilling process is gone through using exactly the same sort of doubler or retort and pewter "worms" as in the early days.

Whether the rum is aged for sale or drunk fairly promptly and fairly 'raw' depends on how one likes his liquor—full of kicks and authority or mellow. These days the new rum is stored in large glass bottles covered in wicker which hold up to 14 gallons each. The stoppers may be made of cane stalks, wood or porous ceramic. It is then aged and sold mostly for local consumption.

BELIEVE IT OR NOT. Rum and Pirates! Everyone thought only the rum remained and all the pirates were gone. But early in 1966 a most startling discovery was revealed on Tortola. If true, it proved the rip-snorting pirate days weren't just a legend after all. For weeks the whole island was talking of a report which came out in the newspaper. The story went like this:

Seven pirates were found! All very dead, and buried neatly in a trench about 38′ long by 18″ deep. The mysterious part was that six of the men were buried in a row head to foot stretched out in the trench, but the seventh was buried at the end to form the shape of a cross or the letter T. The trench ran in a direct north-south line, but just where it was located its discoverers weren't disclosing, except that it was near West End.

The seven sets of human bones involved in what seemed a mass murder were supposedly sent off for laboratory analysis and possible dating. The conjecture went that pirate skullduggery was involved and that the bodies either pointed to treasure or covered it. At last rumor some rather intensive treasure hunting was going on somewhere in all that West End wild acreage.

Then word went around that it was all a hoax.

True or false, who knows? If true, the discoverers have done well to call it a hoax so they will be left in peace to do more digging. If false—well, it was one of the best leg-pullings in Tortola's history, and no harm done. Everyone enjoys a good tale and this one of the pirates' mass murder provided one of Tortola's most stimulating topics of conversation for a long time.

EAST END. On the lovely drive in this direction are a series of spectacular views on the headlands and picturesque small settlements in the valleys. You pass Long Look, home of part of the old Quaker colony on Tortola. It is more fun to walk than to ride through this village and through East End village. Admire the way the East End builders have come to terms with the rocks.

Your car will go on out to the new Queen Elizabeth Bridge which now connects Tortola and its airport-appendage of Beef Island. As you cross the bridge, look down to your left and you may still see the little do-it-yourself pontoon barge which used to hold one automobile and more persons than you could imagine, before the bridge was built. This was pulled back and forth across the channel by means of ropes, pulleys and puffing. Small boys from East End used to loiter there waiting to help haul on the ropes for a small consideration. They are the only ones who regret its demise.

Beef Island isn't impressive to look at, yet you might ponder that it got its name from supplying grazing area for the old buccaneer's cattle back in the late 1600s and early 1700s, and that now there are plans for a hotel and many houses on the island. Past the busy little airport you look across to the quiet little Bellamy Cay in Trellis Bay which at times is a small resort where yachtsmen gather. There are no accommodations on Beef Island itself although some are sure to sprout up eventually to serve air travellers and others.

Look farther out to sea and there is the famed Marina Cay; also a yachtsmen's rendezvous spot.

Looking back northwest you'll see Guana Island, a privately owned island and club. There are also before you Great Camanoe and Little Camanoe close across the channel.

Sit there and wonder what you would have done about all those little islands and reefs if you had been Sir Francis Drake. Even today, chart in hand and with sound devices, some sailors have difficulty figuring it all out.

Beef Island also contains some old Greathouses and sugar factory ruins which are good hiking objectives. For this get local directions before starting, as the ruins are not easy to find.

If you like shelling and swimming where there are no Private signs and probably no one else in sight at all, there is all of Beef Island to choose from. Several good beaches are in the area between the airport beach and the new bridge.

There are many north shore coves and beaches on Tortola which cannot be reached by anything except horseback, mule-back, shank's mare or boat. For these you would need good directions, a map, a full canteen, food and boots. If you don't want to ride horseback or hike over the mountains to those delectable beaches which you glimpse below from the spectacular hilltops, then hire a small boat to take you around the island for the day.

The best swimming on Tortola is on the north shore but the most interesting snorkeling is along the south shore reefs. You can reach lovely beaches by car at Carrot Bay and Cane Garden Bay on the northwest side. Here are two villages which would have delighted Gauguin's eye. They seem straight out of the South Seas when viewed from any distance. The setting is spectacular.

Walk through the villages, talk to the friendly people. If you look sharp you will see an old daub-and-wattle house or two which have withstood time better than some of the old stone mansions. The wattle is woven of hardwood withes, then the cement of white lime and sand is thrown agains the wattle. Here and there where the wattle has worn out, the daub stands alone like a skeleton showing the incised marks of the missing withes.

Don't forget to amble. There is no hurry if you want to really see what you are viewing. Keep an eye open for lonesome little graveyards along the shore or nearby in the brush along the road near the villages. Watch the fishermen sitting on shore mending nets or making those peculiar-shaped lobster traps.

SAGE MOUNTAIN. An excursion to the beautiful rain forest on Sage Mountain high up back of Roadtown is worth the effort, but since you will have to hike in from the road, a guide is suggested. It is not a large forest but an exquisite one containing plants and trees not found elsewhere in this area of the Caribbean. Try to go with someone who can tell you about the tropical growth. You will be at the island's highest point, 1780 feet. It hasn't changed much since the visitor James Smith wrote of it in 1840.

". . . We entered a thick forest, so that we could not see to exceed ten or fifteen feet ahead, unless in the direction of our path. The trees now became large and exceedingly high. What very much attracted our attention was the vines which encircled these trees and ran up them for sixty or seventy feet in height. The leaves on some of these vines were as large as umbrellas. We procured some of them, and the stems which bore them were several feet long. The ladies used them as umbrellas. The forest was silent, very damp and quite cool; after merging from it, our views became most commanding. We could see the principal islands for 50 miles."

Tortola

View from Ruthy Hill

Over Yonder

Everywhere one looks to sea from Tortola, one views other islands, most of them part of the British Virgins. There are the closer appendages named Beef, Bellamy Cay, Little and Great Camanoe, Guana and Marina Cay. Looking on beyond them Scrub is visible and farther east are the small Dogs; West Dog, Great Dog, George Dog and Seal Dogs, named for the howling set up by a heavy surf. Little Cockroach somehow got among the Dogs. Virgin Gorda lies on past the Dogs.

Mosquito Island is topside of Virgin Gorda along with Prickly Pear and Necker Islands. Eustatia is nearby, unfortunately often confused with St. Eustatius which is far to the south of the Virgins.

Stretching south and west from Virgin Gorda is a long arc of islands paralleling Drake's Channel. First is Fallen Jerusalem, obviously named for its tumbled boulders; then next to it is Broken Jerusalem. Next in line are Round Rock, Ginger, Cooper, Salt, Dead Chest, Peter and then Norman Islands. This brings the eye to the closest of the U.S. Virgins, St. John Island, which looms large across Drake's Channel from Tortola.

Near Tortola's West End lie Frenchman's Cay, Little Thatch and Great Thatch. North of them and slightly northwest of Tortola lie the large island of Jost Van Dyke and Little Jost Van Dyke, named so legend says for a famous Dutch pirate. The early explorers and writers had at least ten ways of misspelling the pirate's name, ranging from Josh Vandyke, Josvan Dykes, Gros Van Dikes to Joes Vandicks.

There are more legends and romantic tales than there are islands, many of them probably not at all true, but fascinating as such tales are.

The most famous legend is the one of Dead Chest, celebrated for centuries in the Yo Ho Ho and A Bottle of Rum song. Experts say this is the wrong island for the event, yet local folklore insists that St. Thomas's leading pirate, Blackbeard, whose real name was Teach, marooned fifteen of his men on Dead Chest to try to give them a lesson of sorts about the need for food and water for survival. He stranded them with only a bottle of rum and a cutlass. This island was purchased about twenty years ago by Earl Baldwin and given to the B.V.I. for posterity.

Incidentally, the word marooned entered the language of all the West Indies; often meaning an isolated place for slaves to escape to, as well as the act of being shipwrecked or put ashore by a pirate captain. Back 100 years ago it was fashionable on Tortola to refer to all parties held on or near the water as 'maroons.'

Many of the little islands are skimpy on history but the larger ones have had their moments of wealth, glory or fame.

VIRGIN GORDA. The Fat Virgin, once outshone Tortola as chief island of the Colony. It lies eight miles northeast of Tortola and was the original seat of the government. In 1812 it

reached a peak of 8,000 persons. Its decline was steady and for over a hundred years it had only 600 or less persons living there. Now, with Mr. Laurance Rockefeller's elaborate hostelry of Little Dix Bay flourishing, the people come and go so fast it is difficult to keep count.

The island is about ten miles long with steep hills in the north and central part and low-lying areas elsewhere on two long appendages to the main part of the island. It was named, naturally, by Columbus who thought it resembled a large fat woman lying on her back when seen from the sea.

Virgin Gorda's famous Baths are its greatest attraction for visitors. Here is a spectacular beach area with huge, tumbled and jumbled boulders piled high on each other to the height of a very tall house. The sea washes and rushes in to form cavernous bathing pools inside. The atmosphere and light coloring is limpid, a little melancholy and even forbidding, but with shafts of light pouring in from above is spectacular and dramatic. A sail over from Tortola for a swim in the Baths or at the beautiful beach nearby is well worth the trip. The Baths are open to the public.

Not far off, Spanishtown is the island's main settlement. It is supposedly named for the Spaniards who lived on the island around 1500 but several early writers insist this name is a corruption of the word *penniston*, a type of blue woolen material once used for work clothing for the slaves. It was still being called Penniston as late as 1852.

Spanishtown, or Penniston, the first capital of the colony was Government headquarters in the early 1700's when the island had large estates devoted to ginger, indigo, cattle and sugar cane. Slave labor was the backbone of the system here also until the slave trade and then slavery itself were abolished. After this the estates were gradually abandoned by their owners. Some land went back to 'bush' where it still is; some went to the freed Negroes by purchase or squatters' rights. The island still depends on a small farm economy, but the tourist development is changing this rapidly.

The Spaniards who first settled on Virgin Gorda for short periods in the early 1500s came over from Puerto Rico to mine

74

on Virgin Gorda's southeastern tip of land. These mines were re-opened around 1840 with some 40 miners imported from Cornwall to work them, assisted by about 150 local men. The mining went on until 1867, and one can still see the remains of a crude smelter and ore deposits left from that period. Geologists estimate that more than 10,000 tons of copper ore were taken out altogether by the Spanish and Cornish miners.

The island boasts several topnotch resorts onshore and several smaller ones on the surrounding offshore islands. There are other new facilities, including a large yacht harbour with a shopping centre, which attracts a myriad of private and charter yachts from not only the B.V.I. but also the U.S. Virgins. While Tortola retains a good degree of Britishness, most of these outer islands seem, recently, to have turned more to Americanization; using not only U.S. currency, but many American brand-name products and viewing Stateside television programs. The Americanism which has penetrated deepest is the slang, making for some unusual effects when intermixed with the islanders' soft vernacular.

PETER ISLAND is another comfortable day's sailing excursion from Tortola or Virgin Gorda and a short haul from Norman island also. Most visitors 'do' both in the same day. Peter has two excellent beaches with the traditional palms fringing the shores. There is now an elegant yacht harbour-hotel complex with frequent boat service from Tortola.

Things have not changed too much here since Capt. Thomas Southey, brother of the poet, put down his impressions of it in his *Chronological History Of The West Indies* more than a century and a half ago.

"In May [1806] the author with a party visited Peter's Island, one of those which form the Bay of Tortola, a kind of Robinson Crusoe spot, where a man ought to be farmer, carpenter, doctor, fisherman, planter; everything himself. The owner's house has only the ground floor; a roof of shingles projects some six or eight feet beyond the sides, like a Quaker's hat; not a pane of glass in the house; merely shutters for the apertures. In the centre of the drawing-room or hall, or best room, were triced up ears of Indian corn; on a chair lay a fishing

net; in one corner hung another; a spyglass, fowling piece, chairs, looking glass, and pictures of the four seasons composed the furniture; the library consisted of a prayer-book, Almanack, and one volume of the Naval Chronicle. On the left hand was a room, with a range of machines for extracting the seeds from the cotton. Round the house were abundance of goats, turkeys, fowls, a bull, cow, pigs, dogs and cats. . . ."

"The Old Gentleman was dressed in a large broad-brimmed white hat which appeared to have been in use for half a century; a white night-cap covered his bald head; his blue jacket had lappels buttoned back; his duck waistcoat had flaps down to his knees; the trousers were of the same material as his waistcoat . . . the man leading this isolated life, with only his old wife, who looked more like an Egyptian mummy than anything human, was worth £60,000 . . . he had lived twenty years on that small island and twenty upon Tortola."

This rich old hermit supposedly later went into even deeper seclusion on Norman Island and finished out his life there. What happened to his £60,000 is the basis of some of the treasure stories.

NORMAN ISLAND is also called Treasure Island locally, because, naturally, it has or had treasure. This treasure is documented a little better than most. In 1843, an anonymous author wrote a chatty little book *Letters From The Virgin Islands* in which he told this story:

"Norman, a buccanier, separating himself from his associates, then in force at Anegada, had settled with his portion of the general booty, on this Key. The exclusive claims of Spain to the whole of America, insular and continental, had led, as is well known, to a war of atrocious reprisals between that nation and the other European adventurers. The relative position of the parent states in no way affected this; there was never peace beyond the line! The Spanish *Guard Acostas* continued actively engaged: their orders being to sink, burn and destroy all they met with . . . in a conflict of this kind, Norman and his followers perished—not however, until they had deposited their hoard in that common strongbox, the earth. These premises our friend holds as incontrovertible, the *where* alone remaining."

This anonymous writer may have been behind in the news in his 1843 Letter, as an earlier letter of 1750 written on December 23rd of that year by a "Mr. Fleming" reported "recovery of the treasure from the *Nuestra Senora* buried at Norman Island, comprising 450,000 dollars, plate, cochineal, indigo, tobacco, much dug up by Tortolians." It was the treasure itself, not the *Nuestra Senora* which was buried there! The ship had been wrecked off the coast of North Carolina earlier in the year, having aboard the Governor of Santo Domingo, who may or may not have been making off with a good deal of his island's treasury. The Dominican brought his half million in gold and silver plate along on another ship which was taken by pirates. They eventually buried the treasure on Norman Island. Whether this was Norman's own treasure or he buried still another one there is not clear.

Some die-hards claim that Norman Island is Stevenson's Treasure Island, and some are still digging there now and then. Holes can be seen where an enterprising or hurried seeker took a short cut and blasted for the treasure. There is also a spot on Norman called Treasure Point where there are two caves into which a small boat can enter from the sea. The larger cave has steps carved into the rock, leading to the ledge from which Mr. Fleming supposedly took his treasure.

Except for an occasional curious visitor from a yacht, or tourists over for the day, the bats have the caves and the treasure, if any, to themselves now.

GUANA is one of the few privately owned islands of the group; it is operated as a private club, with its three square miles of 750 acres not generally open to the public. It is so-named because of a rock shaped like the head of an iguana lizard.

MARINA CAY, while privately owned, is a small six-acre island north of Beef which operates a hotel as a popular stopover point for yachts. It also takes in travellers who come without their boats; meeting them at a small dock on Beef Island adjacent to the airport.

TRELLIS BAY has little Bellamy Cay just offshore across from a good beach on Beef Island not far beyond the B.V.I. airport. Bellamy has always been a popular yacht-inn rendezvous spot for sailors heading in or out of Drake's Channel. The beach area on Beef is a convenient departure point for exploring on foot the few old ruins on the island. Once there was a picturesque old shipyard near the beach but that is long gone.

There is a good legend about a resourceful old lady living alone on Beef Island who was much troubled by pirates using Great Camanoe across the channel as a rendezvous point. They had a bad habit of liberating her cattle to make their smoked *boucan*. She sweetly invited them all over for a drink one day. They came gratefully and she gave them one of the 'bush' teas famous in slavery times for doing away with obnoxious masters. Soon she had more dead pirates to dispose of than she could handle.

There is not much else recorded on the history of Great Camanoe, but it has the ruin of one Greathouse on it, the early home of the Quaker Mary Vanderpool. She later married a widower, James Parker, and moved to his home on Guana Island where they lived until 1759. Parker was once chided by the Quaker Meeting for letting his daughter 'marry out' to someone of another faith.

JOST VAN DYKE. This is the island of the Dutch pirate with the many spellings to his name, and it is best remembered as the birthplace of the famous Dr. Lettsom who 'bleeds and sweats 'em.' It once was home for part of the Quaker colony and has a good-sized graveyard on it near the Methodist Church and possibly a Quaker burying-ground.

There is an old ruined fort on the island, and some places with intriguing names: Pull and Be Damm' Point, Pulpit Rock, Man-o'-War Hill, Dim Don Point, Georgy Hole Bay, Boo Point and Reach Hill.

Jost Van Dyke has good beaches at White Bay and Great Harbour. Its population is a little better than average for the outer islands—it has perhaps 200 hardy souls. The interior is rugged, mountainous and challenging. It would provide a good escape for those tired of too much civilization. There are limited accommodations for overnight, food and drinks. One has to arrive by boat, and this outlying island has become a popular stopover point for both charter yachts and local sailors from the U.S.V.I. and B.V.I. Just to the east lies Little Jost van Dyke. Large or little, both these islands are likely to remain *terra-incognita* to most travellers.

The tiny island of Tobago lies near Jost Van Dyke to the west, and is famed for the world's largest blue marlin having been caught in its waters. There is a slightly larger tiny Great Tobago nearby.

SALT ISLAND is noted in early records for a tricky passage by it in from the Caribbean to Sir Francis Drake Channel, and naturally for its three salt evaporation ponds which have been in use for centuries. It still produces a surprising number of pounds of salt annually, but the price has risen considerably from the one shilling per barrel quoted for it in 1845.

SOMBRERO is remembered mostly for the rumpus made when an English captain marooned Robert Jeffreys, a rebellious Armourer's Mate of the Brig *Recruit*, there in 1807 with no food and no water. It is a barren and uninhabited island except for birds and their eggs, which sustain life. When the Admiral heard of the incident he ordered the Captain back to rescue the sailor. Only a shirt and a pair of trousers were found. This so angered the Admiral that he ordered the Captain "out of the country." Later it was confirmed that an American ship had rescued Jeffreys and that he was safe in the United States.

Between Sombrero and Anegada lies a dangerous passage which old sailing directions label "not much frequented by ships."

FALLEN JERUSALEM has excited the imagination of all who have seen it, and several of the early writers set down their impressions. In 1807, the naval surgeon John Waller said it has "a vast series of white rocks, arranged with a kind of regularity in ridges, so as to exhibit to the eye a resemblance of streets and squares and ruined buildings . . . the eye of fancy will survey the remains of ruined temples, columns and arches. These rocks have taken the name of the Fallen City; it is almost impossible to describe the different appearances they assume when viewed from different bearings."

ANEGADA is different too: the off-beat island of the Colony. There are no hills or mountains, no volcanic formations as in all the other islands. It is the local equivalent of a Pacific atoll, and the deadly surrounding reefs are the despair of mariners and chart-makers. The island is totally flat, and has only a few hundred persons residing there.

Anegadans make a living chiefly by going away to make it elsewhere. Air service may change this a little when improvements are carried out on the primitive airport. The local government is working hard to upgrade general conditions there.

Anegada gives the feeling of being anchored, but just barely. Parts of the island are rather water-logged. Above-ground burials are still the custom, with graves built up a few feet instead of down. Its name means drowned or inundated.

Pere Labat, the French Dominican priest who rambled through the West Indies for many years around 1700, says that the Indians used it as an occasional rendezvous, where they got quantities of conch. He saw the massive heaps of shells left by them at the east end of the island.

Labat declared he knew several privateers who had spent months on the island searching for the treasure from a Spanish galleon reputed to be buried there. The privateers had no luck, either the quicksands had swallowed it they thought, or it had been carried off by the devil, who stubbornly refused to allow those to find it who could put it to better use than he would.

The coves and bays provided a lurking place for pirates and buccaneers; Captains Kirke and Bone being said to have often frequented Anegada. A creek on the north side is named for Bone. The pirate Norman once belonged to a group of outlaws here. Only a really knowledgeable sailor could make it through the maze of reefs, and the buccaneers and pirates found the island an ideal hiding place where they were beyond pursuit.

In 1832, the *Journal of the Royal Geographical Society* in

London published the "Remarks on Anegada" written by Robert Hermann Schomburgk, Esq. who had just made soundings of Anegada's passages and charts of the reef. He wrote the keenest observations ever made about the island.

Schomburgk notes that the first settlers following the pirates departure came because they had noted the frequent shipwrecks and had "hopes of advantage to those who might be in the neighborhood to profit by them." These settlers did have a few provision crops, grew a little cotton and reared a little livestock, and they chopped away the undergrowth "full of gum" for sale in St. Thomas.

"The great object, however, always was and still is, the wreck of vessels, and the indolence of the inhabitants is only thoroughly roused by the cry of 'a vessel on the reef!' Scarcely is the news announced, than boats of every description, shallops and sailing vessels, are pushed off with all haste toward the scene of action; arms which have been idle for weeks are brought into exercise and both skill and intrepidity are tasked to the uttermost to get first on board. The scene, indeed, baffles description; and it is to be feared that few are attracted by motives of humanity; some such do exist."

After studying Anegada intensely, Schomburgk found many things unique about it. For one thing much of the island was covered with a grey, silceous and calcareous substance of clay, limestone and vegetable fibres. This sticky, gluey mass swept in with the tide on all but the north shore, and as it hardened had left the imprint of Indian's feet and bird claws.

The writer was impressed with the "shallow ground" which ran underwater from near Anegada, parallel with Tortola's whole northside, almost to Jost Van Dyke. This, said Schomburgk "appears of less depth than it is in reality . . . the bottom is mostly of whitish sand . . . among the superstitions of the inhabitants prevails the tradition that this ground, known by the name of the Middle Ground, rises once a year from its depth to the surface of the water."

The south side of Anegada he found a "continuous mass

of shelves ... intersected with openings, sometimes narrow, sometimes of considerable width and depth." He noted a hollow sound when walking over certain places, and that the only trees on the island grew out of these holes. The west end he found covered with sand and sandy hillocks of such fineness the sand could not be used for mortar. Here in the salt ponds were the flamingos crowded on little isles which resembled oases in a desert. Some of the ponds, he said, produced as much salt annually as 1,500 barrels with the usual price per barrel of one dollar. He was puzzled by one pond in which the bottom sank with men and animals, yet was not of quicksand, and by another piece of elastic ground near White Bay which rose and fell with his footsteps.

"Fresh water is found in great abundance on almost every part of the island, frequently even in the immediate vicinity of the sea and surrounded by salt ponds ... near Loblolly Bay are a range of shelf-holes called 'The Wells' which are filled with fresh water ... formation of the shelf-holes is curious—the mouth is usually from 10 to 25 feet wide and they ascend in the form of a funnel. Fresh water contained in them is said often to rise to an uncommon height, as though forced up by some pressure from beneath, but in general, they ebb and flow with the sea."

"... as there is good anchorage in the vicinity [of the west end], whole fleets might be provided with any quantity they required. I have also been told that this water does not spoil by keeping."

Even more remarkable, said Schomburgk, were the facts that no one on Anegada ever had elephantiasis; that heavy and sudden fogs came up; that in calm and clear weather objects at Virgin Gorda eight miles away "which, at other periods, are entirely invisible, seem to rise above the surface of the water, leaving apparently a vacancy between; and trees, rocks, etc., appear, accordingly, to hover in the air."

Some of the Royal Geographicers must have thought Schomburgk putting it on a bit, but many of the peculiarities of Anegada are just as evident today, and the observer was a trained scientist. The most objectionable thing about the island in 1832 was the huge swarms of giant mosquitos which bothered the

82

residents day and night. A larger species than usual, they were called 'gallon nippers' and the only good thing about them was that now and then they disappeared for as long as ten years. When mounting a full attack they could send the wild goats into the settlements for help. The sheep often died from inflammation and cramps caused by the stings. On the other hand, Anegada was the only island in the area with no cases on record of poisoning from eating fish, which was fairly prevalent elsewhere. Schomburgk was hard put to explain this, but decided it was due to lack of the poisonous machineel trees which often grew with their roots in the sea water around the other islands.

The islanders, he said, hunted the iguana lizards with dogs and had decreased the flamingo flocks greatly because they loved their flesh.

But the chief curiosity about Anegada to Schomburgk was the extraordinary number of shipwrecks around it. He spent much time exploring the reefs and many hours theorizing about this. True, the reefs were utterly deadly for all but experienced sailors to go through, but they were also well charted for all to avoid. Why was it that hundreds of ships, big and small of many nations came to grief on them when the captains thought their ships were far to the south? What caused the errors in reckoning? Schomburgk was the first to realize that the reckonings were right except that something else was wrong. He came to the conclusion that there was a remarkable and large northwest current which sailors and chartmakers did not calculate for or even know about; that this current was strongest from March to June when the trade winds often blew more from the south than southeast.

The seriousness of the problem was confirmed by Schomburgk when he drew up a list of known ships lost on Anegada reefs "within the memory of man." Island residents provided the names, nationality and types of ship for 53 wrecks preceding 1832 along with testimony given by shipwrecked captains who thought they were far from Anegada. Schomburgk drew up some wreck charts himself and proved his theory. Modern sailing charts now allow for this drift, but no one has figured out how to do anything about the reefs.

Today the snorkeler and scuba diver are practically guaranteed some sort of interesting find around the island. After all, for nearly three centuries the inhabitants have been picking up unusual artifacts along the shore after storms, and there must be plenty left in Davy Jones' locker.

Anegada hasn't changed much over the centuries. There have been various plans for major development but the government is moving slowly and carefully on this. There is intermittent boat service in, and one flies in by small private plane, or one can chance the reefs in a sail or motor boat, preferably with a local pilot at the helm. There is a small hotel.

The drowned island still keeps many secrets for the adventurous.

LIVING ON THE ISLANDS. For those willing to do without some of the less necessary amenities of civilization and most of its noise, living on Tortola or one of the other islands can be one of the most satisfactory experiences of a lifetime. More and more visitors are becoming entranced with the British Virgins and soon are enquiring about how to acquire a bit of this paradise. What are the rules to go by? If an outsider feels the urge to own some land here for his Paradise Found or to go into business, the government doesn't forbid it and under certain restrictions welcomes it.

It seems apparent and commendable that what the government doesn't want is speculation which could bring on the sort of inflation of land and other values which has taken place in the nearby U.S. Virgins. Capital investment and orderly development are welcome. The newcomer is required to develop land within an agreed period, spending an agreed minimum rather than to speculate or to just hold on for investment. This policy is guiding the islands toward a controlled development for the best usages of local land and shore resources for residents and tourists alike.

You will be welcome everywhere you go if your manners are as gentle as those of the Tortolans. To generalize—they are quiet, soft-spoken, friendly, honest, hard-working and self-reliant people.

However, don't expect quiet beginning the first Monday in August. Expect instead to join in a week of the gay, carefree and musical times celebrating the day slavery ended.

And, of course, spend at least one day on the water. Engage a day charter and sail along Sir Francis Drake's Channel or across the Channel to Virgin Gorda or any of the dozens of islands radiating out from Tortola where the water is superb for swimming and the beaches beyond compare for lazing. Deep sea fishing enthusiasts will be completely within their element, the catch like the weather is nearly guaranteed.

If you finally have to leave these siren islands and seas, don't forget to return. As the local phrase goes, it should be more than "just a pass by."

Bibliography

Abraham, James Johnston, "Lettsom—His Life, Times, Friends and Descendants." William Heinemann Medical Books Ltd. London, 1935.

Carmichael, Mrs. A. C., "Domestic Manners & Social Conditions of the White, Coloured and Negro Populations of the West Indies." 2 vol. Whittaker & Co. London, 1834.

Chalkley, Thomas, "Collection of Works." Philadelphia, 1749.

Charlevoix, Pierre Francois Xavier de. "A Voyage to North America Undertaken by Command of the Present King of France..." Dublin, 1766.

Davies, John, "The History of the Caribby-Islands...Rendered Into English." (From Rochefort). Dring, London. 1666.

Eadie, Hazel Ballance, "Lagooned in the Virgin Islands." George Routledge & Sons, Ltd. London, 1931.

Edwards, Bryan, "History, Civil & Commercial of the British Colonies of the West Indies." London, 1807.

Fishlock, W. C. "The Virgin Islands. British West Indies Handbook of General Information." 1912.

Government of The British Virgin Islands. "British Virgin Islands, 1961 and 1962 Report," H. M. Stationery Office, 1964.

Government of the British Virgin Islands. "Visit Of Her Majesty, Queen Elizabeth The Second & His Royal Highness Prince Philip, Duke of Edinburgh. Feb. 1966.

Gurney, Joseph John, "Familiar Letters to Henry Clay of Kentucky, Describing A Winter In The West Indies." N.Y., 1840.

Island Sun, The. Newspaper. Roadtown, Tortola, B.V.I., 1966.

Jenkins, Charles F., "Tortola, A Quaker Experiment of Long Ago." Friends' Bookshop. London, 1923.

Kingsley, Charles, "At Last." Harper & Brothers. N.Y., 1871

Knox, John P., "A Historical Account of St. Thomas." Charles Scribner, N.Y., 1852.

"Letters From The Virgin Islands." Anon. Pub. John Van Voorst. London, 1843.

Ober, Frederick A., "In The Wake of Columbus." D. Lothrop & Co. Boston, 1893.

Osborne, John, "Guide To The West Indies." Royal Steam Packet Co. London, 1845.

Pickering, John, "Letter From Tortola," April 10, 1741 to David Barclay, Jr. in London.

Schomburgk, Robert Hermann, "Remarks On Anegada." Journal of Royal Geographical Society. London. July, 1832.

Smith, James, "The Winter of 1840 in St. Croix, With An Excursion to St. Thomas & Tortola." N.Y., 1840.

Southey, Capt. Thomas, "Chronological History of The West Indies." Longman, Rees, Orme, Brown & Green. 3 vol. London, 1827.

Stanton, Daniel, "A Journal of the Life, Travels & Gospel Labours..." Philadelphia, 1772.

Suckling, George, "An Historical Account of the Virgin Islands in the West Indies." Benjamin White, Fleet St. London, 1780.

Truman, George, Jackson, John & Longstreth, Thomas B. "Narrative of A Visit To The West Indies in 1840-41." Philadelphia, 1827.

Waller, John Augustine, "Voyage In The West Indies...". Sir Richard Phillips & Co. London, 1820.

"West India Sketch Book," Anon. Whittaker & Co. London, 1834.

"West Indies Directory, Gulf of Mexico & West India Islands." James Imray & Sons. London, 1878.